Sandbox Strategies for the New Workplace

SANDBOX STRATEGIES FOR THE NEW WORKPLACE

Conflict Resolution from the Inside Out

PENNY TREMBLAY

ROWMAN & LITTLEFIELD
Lanham • Boulder • New York • London

Published by Rowman & Littlefield
An imprint of The Rowman & Littlefield Publishing Group, Inc.
4501 Forbes Boulevard, Suite 200, Lanham, Maryland 20706
www.rowman.com

86-90 Paul Street, London EC2A 4NE

British Library Cataloguing in Publication Information Available

Library of Congress Cataloging-in-Publication Data

Names: Tremblay, Penny, 1976– author.
Title: Sandbox strategies for the new workplace : conflict resolution from the
  inside out / Penny Tremblay.
Description: Lanham : Rowman & Littlefield, [2023] | Includes bibliographical
  references and index.
Identifiers: LCCN 2022060771 (print) | LCCN 2022060772 (ebook) |
  ISBN 9781538170212 (cloth) | ISBN 9781538170229 (epub)
Subjects: LCSH: Conflict management. | Communication in organizations. |
  Interpersonal relations.
Classification: LCC HD42 .T73 2023 (print) | LCC HD42 (ebook) |
  DDC 658.4/053—dc23/eng/20230109
LC record available at https://lccn.loc.gov/2022060771
LC ebook record available at https://lccn.loc.gov/2022060772

CONTENTS

Foreword by Samuel Dinnar vii

Preface: Why Conflict Surfaces in Most Workplaces xi

CHAPTER 1 Position Yourself for Success 1

CHAPTER 2 Lighten Your Load 21

CHAPTER 3 Actively Listen 39

CHAPTER 4 Yield to Your WHY 55

CHAPTER 5 Nurture Relationships 69

CHAPTER 6 Include Everyone 85

CHAPTER 7 Challenge Conflict 101

CHAPTER 8 Empathize 119

Conclusion: Keeping These Eight Strategies Top of Mind 131

Notes 137

Index 145

Acknowledgments 153

About the Author 155

FOREWORD

*By Samuel Dinnar, conflict resolution expert
and negotiation teacher at Harvard and MIT*

I MET PENNY YEARS AGO AT HARVARD, WHEN SHE WAS GOING through some her life's most challenging transitions, but also some of her most rewarding moments of growth and purpose. There she was, one of forty-eight experienced mediators from around the globe who came to our Harvard Negotiation Institute to learn about advanced mediation and resolving complex disputes. These amazing diverse peacemakers were all challenging themselves to learn and share knowledge, striving to do a better job in helping others in their communities. We all felt the common human purpose of being dedicated to making the world a better place.

I remember teaching one particular class that week, where I shared my emotional experience from a company dispute where everything was on the line. Losing would mean shutting down the company and firing all the employees who put years of their lives to making it succeed. The stakes couldn't be higher. We then moved to a hands-on exercise, an in-class role-play simulation to experience how to help parties resolve such a heated complex conflict. The role-playing allowed some universal truths to emerge about how in business (and in life) conflict is inevitable, and how working through conflict can uncover significant value and also improve relationships. A lively discussion afterward also helped clarify how the dangerous alternative of not resolving the dispute could lead to a disaster. We explored various moves and mediation techniques and gleaned some valuable lessons before asking for volunteers to try it again, in front of the class (in what we call a fishbowl role-play). I recall how Penny went beyond her comfort zone to take on the role of one of the disputants, and how later, in the middle of the attempts to reach resolution, she explained what she was feeling. She vividly articulated how a part of her wanted to fight, a part of her wanted to flee, and yet another part wanted to resolve this matter and move on. Penny helped us all learn while displaying great empathy and awareness.

I have tracked Penny's progress since then. How she continued to improve her skills and expand her coaching, training, and mediation offerings. She intimately knows the subject matter and how to communicate with people, and has helped hundreds of individuals and groups to resolve their conflicts and improve their relationships. I was honored when she asked me to write the foreword for this book.

During my career as a business executive, entrepreneur, investor, and consultant, I have seen the ups of down of business dealings. I've been fortunate to be part of companies and collaborations that have led to great new world-changing products and billion-dollars businesses. Unfortunately, I have also seen many millions of dollars of value destroyed at the negotiating table and in the workplace, due to egos and emotions, resulting in innovations lost, opportunities missed, employees suffering toxic environments, and companies shut down. I have learned how critical managing good relationships is, and how productive a team that plays well together can be.

I assume that you are living through conflict right now.

I can make that assertion because life is full of conflicts. In business, in the community, and at home, your interests are somewhat different than those of your colleagues, neighbors, or loved ones. Ignoring those difference does not solve the problems. Whether you share the same space or interact over phone or email, you will need to communicate to bridge those differences and come to a better understanding and some workable solution. But how should you go about it? How can you bring yourself and the other party to have that discussion? How can you make that discussion a success?

This book provides an accessible and manageable way to approach these important questions. Penny created a memorable framework for how to PLAY NICE with your colleagues and other people in your life. She presents her ideas and personal stories with honesty, clarity, and even productive vulnerability. She has curated vivid examples from workplace and family relationships that illustrate each recommended approach, along with references to concepts from subject matter experts who have helped her and her clients over the years. She illustrates time and again how we can all be better off working through conflict instead of trying to go around it, and provides a clear list of eight strategies starting with one's own self, moving to communication methods, and delving into interpersonal dynamics.

This book takes into consideration the new reality of a postpandemic world. COVID-19's impact was significant. The world changed, including the world of business. In-person relationships transitioned to online, and we all had more time to reflect on our own behaviors and relationships. We felt and saw how working remotely increases miscommunications, worsens misunderstandings, and leads to more conflict in the workplace.

Don't be fooled by the book's title and leading metaphor. *Play nice in the sandbox* may evoke a simple childhood image where everything is rosy and easy, but Penny clearly goes deep and extends this metaphor to beyond childlike play. She'll remind you that at any age, we carry with us our challenges to let go of longtime habits and the defense mechanisms that we acquired earlier in our life or our career. While Penny uses a simple list of eight strategies, she will vividly walk you through how to reflect on your own life, how to implement people skills (that are not easy to implement alone), and how to practice interpersonal interactions in order to continuously improve. Use this book to learn and practice. Better yet, share this learning process with a coach or a buddy. Your reward is guaranteed to be huge.

Samuel Dinnar

- Harvard Negotiation Institute instructor of mediation and conflict resolution
- Negotiation and Leadership instructor at the Program on Negotiation (PON) at Harvard Law School
- Lecturer of engineering leadership and negotiation at Massachusetts Institute of Technology (MIT)
- Business advisor and mediator at Meedance
- Coauthor with Larry Susskind of the award-winning book *Entrepreneurial Negotiation: Understanding and Managing the Relationships That Determine Your Entrepreneurial Success*

PREFACE

Why Conflict Surfaces in Most Workplaces

Where there is human interaction, there will always be conflict; however, suffering is optional. —Penny Tremblay

DO YOU SUFFER THE BURDEN OF UNRESOLVED CONFLICT?
Initially, most people I work with who are suffering the effects of conflict blame other people and wish they'd just get their "shift" together and play nice! But permanent conflict resolution requires that we take responsibility for the difficulties we encounter and use skills the educational system never taught us.

Case in point: Mary. The general manager of her office job continued to harass her until she filed a formal complaint. Or at least that's the way she thought of the situation. As she later described what was happening, I began to see things a little differently:

"And another time," Mary continued with a third example of what she called one of these harassing situations that made her uncomfortable, "I'd started out of the office for lunch, leaned down to grab my wallet out of the bottom drawer, and my boss says, 'Just take your time down there; it's a great view.'"

Mary looked at me as if she'd made her point.

"I don't get it," I said. "You mentioned that he'd just told you that you looked stressed and that it was fine to take a few extra minutes for lunch whenever you needed it. And you said that people often stroll down around the Riverwalk because the view down there is relaxing."

"Yeah. But that's not what he meant! He was referring to the view of my backside when I bent over!"

"Are you sure? You have to consider the context of your whole conversation."

"Look, it was a suggestive comment. I know what he meant! It was vulgar."

I didn't argue the point with Mary, but instead let her give me other examples that she considered offensive, harassing, intimidating. Definitely, she felt deep conflict and hurt.

So the upshot of Mary's conflict with her boss and the formal conflict she'd filed?

The conclusion of a $20,000 workplace investigation cost to the company, which stalled the department for six months, found no harassment. And the workplace culture was deeply affected.

I was called in to restore their poisoned culture to peace and productivity with my Sandbox System™. I met with Mary for the conversation (part of which I described above), where I listened with the intention of understanding her perspective. We talked about many things, including her four-year term with the current company, her aspirations, her family life, and her employment history. Then I asked the question, "Have you ever been harassed before?"

There was a long pause before her answer.

"Yes." Mary's gaze dropped. She responded as if in shame. "I was sexually harassed by my former employer."

"I'm sorry to hear that, Mary." I said. "How long ago did that happen?"

"Twenty years ago ..." She proceeded to share the story of a formal complaint that she'd filed, which resulted in a full investigation, criminal charges, and repercussions for the violator. After the incident, she had decided to leave the organization, to take several years off before joining her current team.

It never ceases to amaze me how current conflict almost always has links to the past, yet these links seem hidden from those entangled in their mess of emotional baggage (which I refer to as one's "suitcase"). Mary, thankfully, saw the link too. She was honest and vulnerable enough to see her part in the battle. She was speaking and listening to her new boss from the perspective of a twenty-year-younger, sexually harassed victim.

I met with the new general manager who had joined the company just six months prior to the investigation to understand his perspective, communication style, and challenges. He had no idea of Mary's backstory until they came together for a face-to-face conversation with intention to resolve their differences and make new commitments on how best to work together.

Within a short hour of my mediation process, Mary decided to share her vulnerable story with her general manager. A melding of human empathy was happening right before my watery eyes. His ears could hear her honesty. His eyes could see her vulnerability. His soul could feel her pain.

The authentic conversation moved him to feel two things: relief that he was not the root cause of Mary's presumptions, plus empathy for Mary. He decided on his own to make accommodations for the way Mary needed to be treated at work. They connected in those minutes of conversation, and both agreed to form new commitments for the benefit of their working relationship and the organization.

The happy ending seemed like it would have lasting impact, but it had an unusual twist. It did not stick. After a few months, Mary resigned for what she thought were greener pastures, and landed a job elsewhere. But the new job didn't last. She was terminated before her three-month probation period, because this latest employer was onto her behaviors early. Mary is still speaking and listening from her past, which is wreaking havoc on her future career.

HOLY SHIFT! This high cost of conflict—emotional, time, and dollars—is avoidable.

Most Conflict Resolution Is an Inside Job

Conflict is costly. Can you imagine the time and money that could be put to better use if people found peace with their unresolved past and learned to embrace future conflict as an opportunity to learn and grow?

As a workplace-relationships expert helping remote and on-site teams resolve conflict for the last couple of decades, I've learned that there's only one way through conflict, and that's through it. You can't go over it, under it, or around it. You must go through the discomfort, to get to the other side where peace, personal growth, and profitable lessons from the uncomfortable process make it all worthwhile. But most people avoid the discomfort of conflict and stay stuck in the suffering, not knowing the way out.

Playing **nice doesn't always mean** *being* **nice.** Finding your assertive voice, speaking up, and setting your boundaries are resolution tools that are everyone's right—yet highly underutilized.

NOW is prime time to reimagine thriving in your best career, workplace, or business, because the grains of sand have shifted during the pandemic era. Despite the fact that we're in a perfect sandstorm for conflict, this new landscape is rich with opportunity for change.

The Grains of Sand Have Shifted

Do you remember making castles in the sand? How about your return to the sandbox the following day to find all your efforts leveled or turned into something that you hadn't anticipated? This is what COVID-19 has done to businesses everywhere. It has washed away what was and has brought new opportunity to create again. But this time, we have more knowledge of what was working as well as what wasn't, and the opportunity to create a solid foundation for future growth. The essence of sand is impermanence, because nothing is ever set in sand.

COVID-19 has not changed our future. It has accelerated it.

The book manuscript I had ready in early 2020 now lines my wastepaper basket, because although workplace conflict was already a $359 billion cost to North American organizations before COVID-19, that number pales in comparison to conflict costs postpandemic, even despite remote working.

Organizations have been either ripped apart with displaced employees in remote working arrangements or pressured to work together separated by plexiglass in an ever-changing environment. We've become more disconnected than ever.

The human cost of stress-related conflict and high anxiety touches each of us personally. Our poor mental health and overall wellness stemming from the inner turmoil fueled by conflict is a huge price to pay.

Survey Says . . .

Our Tremblay Leadership Center recently analyzed over 550 global survey responses from managers and employees to determine the effects of COVID-19 on workplace conflict. Key findings reveal that conflict has increased since the pandemic began and includes much of the common workplace conflicts that we were previously experiencing plus many additional challenges.[1] To note:

- Nearly two-thirds of office-work employees are now working from home, which makes one's new "workplace" their home sandbox.
- Managing people remotely requires a new set of tools to close the communication gap and create the connection they're craving from not being together physically.
- Working in-office or remotely presents consistent challenges of increased workloads, decreased communication, and a resistance to embrace change at such a rapid pace.
- Employees report high levels of conflict brewing that managers do not yet recognize or acknowledge. (This revelation feels like finding a cat turd buried beneath the sandy surface!)

The perfect storm for conflict, its cost to organizations, as well as the stress and burnout to those involved, lurks overhead.

Other escalating conflict indicators from our research include insecurity, conflicting values, and resistance to change, all which are fueling the typical high stress of interpersonal relationships at work and beyond.

With so many employees now working from home—which many corporate executives indicate is a shift that may be permanent—we anticipate the high corporate cost of conflict to increase. Employees are struggling with juggling remote work arrangements, the health crisis, and limited trust from working in isolation. Although communication with managers may have increased since the pandemic began, physical distance erodes trust in relationships. Time spent in isolation brings on feelings of exclusion, so we're left sitting in our own messy thoughts that we used to blame on others we've labeled as "difficult." That lack of trust means more and more people hesitate to speak up due to recent political divisions with governments, races, and even vaccination opinions!

The good news? Because most conflict resolution is an inside job, **you** can use the following eight sandbox strategies to PLAY NICE and build your greatest castle.

Playful Conflict Resolution

These tools help people become responsible, influential, and productive problem solvers. They'll help you embrace and even welcome conflict with coworkers, bosses, clients, and others. Healthy teams embrace conflict. Healthy relationships discuss and grow from conflict. In this book, you'll learn to master the eight PLAY NICE strategies to exponentially increase your capacity to:

- Embrace, accept, and welcome conflicting values
- Understand the importance of collaborative relationships for career advancement
- Take responsibility to cocreate a winning culture with productive and profitable results
- Empathize with coworkers and even competitors to be the leader others WANT to follow

The eight sandbox strategies contained in the chapters of this book turn conflict resolution inside out and make it a work of play. They're illustrated with rich anecdotes, relevant analogies, and fun examples of tools (toys) that you'll recall in your early days. Shovels and castles, sand sieves and bulldozers, watering cans, army figures, shade umbrellas, and more. These "conflict" lessons are as creative and constructive as the childhood sandbox:

Position yourself for success. Good play starts within.
Lighten your load. Unpack to make space for new relationship tools.
Actively listen. Help others feel understood.
Yield to your WHY. Ground yourself in purpose.

Nurture relationships. People who feel valued perform well.
Include everyone. Everyone wants to feel part of the whole.
Challenge conflict. Healthy teams learn to embrace it.
Empathize. Balance people's personal needs and business needs.

Although conflict is not new but now amplified, the tools to resolve our current issues are different from the prepandemic period. Some old tools and some new ones are needed, and like the excitement of a child playing with new toys and old favorites, this book will bring you a playful approach to conflict resolution relevant to the new workplace.

An Essential Tool Kit for the New Workplace

Are you a person who wants to play hard, make a positive impact, and climb the corporate ladder with a feeling of team unity—but find yourself in a toxic sandbox that's sucking the life out of you?

Do you avoid conflict rather than confront it head-on?

Are you a business owner or manager who just wants people to really "show up" to the shift schedule they committed to and perform as well as their résumé said they could?

Do you blame and feel resentment toward others for their behavior?

As companies seek economic viability to rebuild their diminished workforce and allocate profits to better use, a tool kit to play nice in this new workplace sandbox is essential for all involved.

The proverbial advice to managers rings true once again: People have always been hired for their technical skills but fired or stuck in their career due to their inability to maintain good relationships—especially when the going gets tough. People join companies, but they quit managers.

Many employees are reexamining, redesigning, and redefining their lives. That means they're taking a serious new look at who they work for, where, when, and how. Challenges surrounding the maintenance of a strong team is no longer termed a worker shortage, but rather a worker shortage *crisis*.

This new virtual, global sandbox presents a playing field that requires a different set of tools. As we embark on this new way of building an economy, the strategies and tools to excavate, cultivate, elevate, and duplicate one's greatest castle are contained within these pages.

HOLY SHIFTS!

While reading this book, you will have enlightening moments that can shift your mind and behavior for better relationships. I call these moments "HOLY SHIFTS." These points of awareness are powerful opportunities to make lasting personal and professional progress. Pay attention to these moments. Anytime you feel the poke, the nudge, the bolt of enlightenment—when you read something, and you know it can shift your way of being—write it down as an actionable item to work on. There is a worksheet download to collect these ideas for action referenced at the back of this book with information about the author and our Sandbox Training programs.

You can also say, "HOLY SHIFT" anytime you want to shift an old way of thinking. Remember, everything you do begins with a thought, so when you don't feel good about your thought, try saying, "HOLY SHIFT" and choose a different thought.

Peaceful, productive, and profitable relationships are your responsibility. Let's dig in with new tools!

The Workplace Sandbox

Do you throw sand?

The early skill sets we build in the sandbox include social skills, collaborative skills, and the acceptance of impermanence, because nothing is ever set in sand. Socially, we learned to share toys and small spaces and to take turns. Collaboration, negotiation, and problem solving were important for those little roadway projects and the villages we built, and we also learned about the constant shape shifting that sand does; castles can flop over, water dissolves what once was into a mud puddle, yet we learned to enjoy things in the moment and then create something more incredible next time.

We understand "PLAY NICE in the sandbox" as a playful metaphor that symbolizes timeless principles of caring, sharing, and working together, which is nice and easy when things are smooth, but how do you manage difficult situations with people?

Do you make intimidating mud patties and serve them to your colleagues?

Do you typically pick up your toys and go home?

I've asked many people about their early experiences in the sandbox. The answers ranged from memories of comparison, equality, fairness, and jealousy, to bullies, competition, and someone stomping on their castle ... to the need to be the winner, king of the sandcastle, owner of the most toys, or the one who gets his or her own way, to the quality of the sand and lack of resources, space, toys, and sand itself. Some people don't remember ever being invited to play, while others said they got sand in places they didn't care to admit. We can certainly relate all these same issues to the adult sandbox of today's workplaces. Comparison and competition, wanting to win, to have the most and best resources, to have fun and build productively, and perhaps the only difference is the profitability we all seek in playing at the game of work.

There's not much difference between the way we were taught to play nice in the early sandbox and playing nice in an adult workplace sandstorm—I mean sandbox—but we all can go into "childish thinking" pretty quick when things get tough, and this creates stress, conflict, and potential loss of relationships with good people.

Decades ago, when I went to work every morning, I'd pump myself up to have the greatest day ever, and even if the sun was shining, the birds were chirping, and the day started out great, when I walked in the doorway of that workplace, the energy was so heavy, it felt like I was being sucked through the floor.

People who were supposed to be in on time weren't, or they'd called in sick, or would be off on stress leave (FMLA). I'd go to the coffee station, hoping for a cup of inspiration, only to hear gossip and negativity. Back at my desk, I'd put out a few new fires, mostly conflicts between staff or managers, and I would wish that people would just show up and do the jobs they'd signed up for—the jobs they were being paid for.

Witnessing and feeling the effects of disconnected relationships and unresolved conflicts, I wanted to go home, and it was only 9:15 a.m.!

Can you relate to this? Are you working in a negative workplace? Are you a person who wants to feel joy, play hard, and make an impact, but your workplace sandbox is a toxic environment that's sucking the life out of you and not healthy for you to play in? Do you sometimes wish that people would just get their "*shift*" together and PLAY NICE?

In the years since I experienced working in a toxic workplace, I've been digging into conflict resolution, mediation, and full workplace restorations. I now understand solutions for workplace conflict, team dysfunction, lack of productivity, lack of team engagement, lack of retention, and how to reduce stress from mismanaged relationships. It is my mission to write, speak, and teach people how to *play nice* in the workplace sandbox, and when they don't, I help them fix broken relationships.

Relationships are fascinating to me. They're the juice that attracts people to each other, makes them want to spend time together, and to live and work cohesively and collaboratively. These workplace sandbox strategies will provide you with new and current ability to playing nice when the going gets tough. It's a skill set that will help you to deal with people in challenging circumstances in a way that exponentially increases the likelihood of:

- Resolving conflicts
- Maintaining connected workplace relationships
- Staying focused on the work that you were hired to do
- Attaining productive, peaceful, and profitable results
- Cocreating a winning culture
- Advancing your career as a leader that others WANT to follow

Sandbox Strategies for the New Workplace is the title I chose because everyone understands the metaphor, and readers think, "Sandbox—fun—let's play!" The caveat here is that it's easier said than done, especially since the pandemic has shifted attitudes and priorities.

When I teach groups how to *PLAY NICE* in the sandbox, people are usually quite sure that they fall into the *NICE* category, and they are quite eager for me to call out the naughty ones who don't play nice in the sandbox. Right? I mean let's be honest . . . the workplace would be so much better if it weren't for OTHER people!

Here's some irony about me. I have based my career and life's work on the topic of rich relationships and conflict management. I've studied at Harvard, researched for years, written extensively on the subject, and spent most of my waking hours immersed in the study and application of restoring workplace conflict to harmony and productivity, and yet in recent years I have faced challenges and adversity in my own relationships that have put all my theories to the test. In 2014, my long-term partner and I separated, my family broke apart, and it took me years to pick up the pieces. It was a defining moment—an opportunity to walk my talk and put my own *PLAY NICE* skills to the test.

Why am I telling you this? It's important to know that I'm not here just because I'm an expert on the subject or trained and spoken to thousands of people. I'm here because I've had my share of relationship struggles, and just like you, I am still learning to play nice through challenging circumstances. Relationships can be hard, no matter who you are. When everything is easy, it's easy, but when we are challenged, we don't always do the right thing. Case in point: when Will Smith smacked Chris Rock at the Academy Awards. One wrong move influenced his entire future. Physical, verbal, mental, or emotional abuse is intolerable today.

Conflict is inevitable in our lives, but suffering is optional. Avoidance is not a solution. Most people avoid conflict because it has an awkwardness or discomfort about it. Even the word itself sounds like combat, but the truth is that healthy teams and partnerships embrace conflict because it makes them stronger.

As you increase your ability to get through challenging times in the best possible way, you will be increasing your "sandbox factor." The first steps to conflict resolution at work belong to the individuals who are at odds with each other. The employer's role is significant, grounded in workplace culture development designed to prevent conflict among employees to the extent possible. The primary onus lies with each one of us, to be responsible (response-able) for our actions, our attitudes, and the results that we want from our careers.

The State of Workplace Conflict during COVID-19

Our 2021 organic research of 550 respondents in Canada and the United States uncovered the highest stressors and the types of conflict that plagued performance during the COVID-19 pandemic period.[2]

Workplace conflict has increased despite remote working. Fifty-five percent of respondents indicated that there is more conflict in the workplace currently than there was prepandemic, even though over 63 percent of respondents were not physically going into a workplace.

We found that people are avoiding appropriate attempts to work through the conflict that is brewing among employees of all levels in the organization, and that employees are pressured by their workload, but they aren't talking about it to their managers. These hidden red flags induced by workload and personal demands will result in the next organizational epidemic of burnout if not addressed promptly.

Key Findings

The old expression that "distance erodes trust" couldn't be more true as we aren't gathering around the boardroom table as much (or ever), with so many office workers serving remotely. Thirty percent of those who responded felt unstable about their job, stemming from lack of communication and social disconnection. Forty-four percent would feel safer with new policies for safety at work.

Current Workplace Conflict Trends

When asked what types of conflict were currently present in their workplace, people indicated these types, ordered by popularity (only 22 percent of respondents indicated that there was no known conflict present in their organization):

- People resistant to change—40 percent
- Negativity causing a decrease in morale—38 percent
- Complaints about workload fairness—37 percent
- People taking things personally—32 percent
- Coworkers who do not get along—23 percent

Common causes of interpersonal conflicts were recorded as:

- Communication styles—63 percent
- Personality differences—45 percent
- Conflicting values—31 percent
- Envy—15 percent
- Competition for promotions—11 percent

Conflict about Workloads Fills the Stress Bucket

The highest increase of conflict is hiding in circumstances surrounding workload, workspace, and family members as people tried to settle into new habits that were interrupted by consistent change.

Stress topped the scale of troubles indicated, followed by isolation, time management/work-life balance, lack of communication, and feeling excluded. It's not only internal conflict that workers are managing. Fifty-four percent of those surveyed indicated that their customers were more difficult to deal with, adding to stress levels that reach beyond the organization's control.

Workers Aren't Hitting Conflict Head-On

With all the conflict going on, 40 percent of respondents talk about it to their supervisor, and 13 percent don't talk about it at all. Our resolution skills are not improving with distance, because fewer face-to-face conversations are taking place to work through issues. Methods used to resolve issues are lacking in interpersonal connection. Thirty-three percent use email, 22 percent hope their supervisor will take care of it for them, 11 percent use text messages, and 8 percent avoid it altogether.

Are We Thriving or Just Surviving?

Although it may seem that we have survived two years of pandemic upheaval, trends in workplace conflict indicate that we are not thriving. COVID-19 hasn't gone away, things are constantly changing, and there is more conflict brewing under the surface that managers are going to want to root out and resolve.

Employee Workload Issues Are
Not Recognized by Managers

When separating employee from manager responses, we recognized that conflict regarding workload and resources were popular with employees, yet unknown to managers. Although employees claim to have little conflict with their managers and colleagues, there is a storm brewing and not communicated through the chain of command, relating to employee work-life balance issues and burnout.

Burnout Is the Next Epidemic

Just as researcher and author Jennifer Moss was proving that prepandemic burnout was getting worse and that people were working themselves sick, 2.6 billion people went into lockdown due to the pandemic, and 81 percent of the workplaces globally closed. The scramble to work from home and manage with Zoom, or double down in a front-line worker role made burnout much worse. "We need to get out ahead of this. Not only does ignoring [burnout] claim too many financial costs, but the human costs are unacceptable."[3]

Now more than ever, workplaces are challenged by stress, mental health issues, retaining talent, and the capacity to work through conflict.

Stress and Mental Health

The fact that people are hired for their technical skills but fired or stuck in dead-end positions due to their lack of ability to get along with people is still true today, but there are additional issues. Mental health, and stress in particular, is a challenge both for employers and employees. The biggest contributing factor to workplace stress is mismanaged relationships.

According to Mental Health Commission of Canada statistics,[4] the biggest contributing factor to days lost due to mental health is workplace stress. One in five Canadians experiences a mental health problem or illness each year, equating to five hundred thousand employees unable to work every week due to mental health problems or illnesses.

What we can influence is how we deal with workplace stress. Rather than people picking up their toys and going home (fleeing, abandoning, alienating, suing, or medicating), we can talk about it. What doesn't help is our addiction to digital communication and our habits of shallow, surface connection that breeds a disconnection. We avoid difficult conversations, unfriend or ghost people with the click of a button, and seem to have amassed a huge army of "keyboard warriors" who hide behind their screens and lash out. The more connected we seem as a human race, the more disconnected we are becoming as a society.

Why People Leave

Although so much of the "great resignation" media discussion is focused on a dissatisfaction of wages, workplace data and over a million Glassdoor reviews were assessed in an *MIT Sloan Management Review* article,[5] which ranked compensation as sixteenth among other topics predicting turnover. Although pay had a more moderate influence on employee decision to leave (except in nursing and large health care systems), **a toxic corporate culture was identified as the highest predictor of attrition** in Culture 500 companies from April through September 2021. The article indicated that elements contributing to a toxic workplace culture include failure to promote DEI (diversity, equity, and inclusion); workers feeling disrespected; and unethical behavior. The remaining four of the top five reasons were identified as job insecurity and reorganization, high levels of innovation, failure to recognize employee performance, and poor response to COVID-19.

According to a study analyzing twenty-five thousand employees, *Inc.* magazine lists the top five reasons why people leave as:[6]

1. Poor management performance
2. Lack of employee recognition
3. Overworked employees
4. Company culture not a priority
5. No growth opportunities

According to *Forbes*,[7] people don't typically quit jobs—they quit managers and/or teams, or leave toxicity for something healthier.

The average cost of losing an employee to turnover is 33 percent of their salary. That's a lot of potential for increased profit being forfeited. Good people are worth investing in and keeping. Being a good employee is also worth striving for, because everyone is better off when relationships are maintained, but let's face it, conflict is inevitable.

The Cost of Conflict

According to a 2008 CPP Global Human Capital Report,[8] employees spend on average 2.8 hours per week dealing with conflict. That's 385 million working days lost, which calculates to $359 billion of unproductive hours paid, lost time, lost productivity, poor decisions, toxic cultures, worker turnover, reputational damage, and legal costs, which are substantial. That number pales in comparison to the NEW workplace conflict. For years I've asked audiences if they thought the statistic of 2.8 hours per week was an accurate representation for them, and 90 percent agreed that it was too low. Then the pandemic hit. As indicated in our research, conflict and stress increased tremendously. Ouch! And all players should be saying, "Ouch!" because great teamwork and collaboration is everyone's responsibility, and profits can be used for better things. Not only is conflict costly, but the stress is killing us.

Restoring peace is a highly sought-after commodity; building teams that are resilient with skills to embrace conflict offers the competitive edge that today's sensitive economy demands. Healthy teams learn to embrace conflicts about systems and processes, and they take responsibility to resolve personality conflicts.

The Round Sandbox

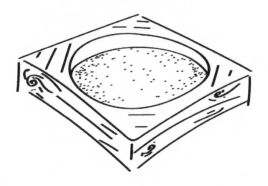

This model took shape one day while I was working for an Indigenous group. I handed Elder Gordon Waindubence[9] my business card, and he studied it for what seemed like a long time before he stated, "Our [Indigenous] sandbox is round." Now, this was great feedback. In over a decade of serving many Indigenous and non-Indigenous work teams with healing circles, I've discovered the value of the circle as a format to hold conversations. The origin of mediation actually came from Indigenous tribal leaders thousands of years ago who used the circle to bring people together to resolve social conflict. "Yes! A circle," I affirmed. Of course, a circle symbolizes UNITY; it has no beginning or end. It's equal. The power of the sandbox IS round.

Here's why. You're more likely to play nice face-to-face. You don't turn your back, retreat to your corner, work in your silos, or stay silent all day. You get in the game, you get inside the box, and you position yourself to play nice, play hard, play well, play fair, play together . . . one team, one mission . . . and that is the foundation of connectedness. The first step to PLAY NICE in the sandbox is to Position Yourself for Success.

I

Position Yourself for Success

Good play starts within.

How do you define leadership?

I define leadership as leading yourself and others . . . in that order. To make a positive impact or be influential externally, we must do our own internal work first. It's thinking inside the box. It's human nature to want to come out big—to have a powerful self-disposition or present ourselves as larger than life in conversations, relationships, and success. However, to come out big, we must go in first, even though our instincts tell us otherwise. Positioning ourselves for good play is not about adjusting body language or holding firm to a mental position or idea. It's about positioning ourselves as authentic, confident, and influential people. The body language will follow our internal disposition.

Let's use the example of my favorite pro golfer, my son Ryan. He wants to get the ball as far as possible down the fairway, toward, and into, the hole with the least number of strokes. To drive that ball two or three hundred yards, he needs to come out big off the tee. His first motion, however, is not toward the hole. Instead, he draws his club into a full backswing, only then bringing it forward to connect with the ball and drive it much farther than if he'd just teed up and swung forward. So it is with baseball: the pitcher goes opposite direction first. The batter goes the opposite direction first, then BAM . . . home run!

This is also true with the game of life. To come out big on the outside, we need to go in, polish up our own perception of ourselves, and clean up old junk that we're carrying around. From my decades of experience helping individuals and work teams resolve conflict, I have noted time and time again that so much of conflict resolution is an inside job. This internal polishing is what I refer to as "positioning ourselves for success."

Taking responsibility for your own personal leadership is a mental shift, a HOLY SHIFT, a responsibility to bring your best authentic self to work. It's not ego. It's not thinking that you're better than you are, or better than others. It's being real, human, and humble enough to be honest about all that you are and know what you're not. It's turning your stumbling blocks into humbling blocks and recognizing YOUR work to become that world-class performer, like Ryan. Without the right positioning, you won't drive the distance, and you'll get stuck in sand traps and lose your balls to the water holes.

Build Your Sandcastle First

Positioning yourself for good play requires an awareness of what you're bringing (or not bringing) to the workplace sandbox. With a willing-ness and openness to see what needs to be seen in ourselves, we won't be looking to others for change, or saying, "Not me . . . I don't throw sand, or bury turds, or steal people's toys, or pick mine up in a huff and go home."

Personal leadership is foundational to professional development. You can't build a castle on quicksand. Your self-worth is critical to your ability to be well positioned for success. Turning inward and thinking inside the box to discover things in YOU that aren't allowing peace and productivity is a worthwhile investment. Be honest and vulnerable about this quest to test the foundation of your esteem and confidence. If you find a lack of integrity, vulnerability, or weakness, you can rebuild it so that you'll be able to build your castle on level ground.

Brain Science

Daniel Amen, MD, author of *Change Your Brain, Change Your Life*, explains that the brain is like a computer with both hardware (physical function) and software (programming). Neither are separate from each other, and therefore the ongoing programming and reshaping over our lives can have a dramatic impact on each other. In "brain SPECT imaging" (single-photon emission computed tomography), which looks at blood flow and activity patterns, many important life lessons are being learned about the brain. An exciting lesson he has learned is that we can literally create change with brain-healthy habits, one of which is correcting negative beliefs. He did a brain scan on himself at the age of thirty-seven and found a toxic, bumpy appearance. All his life he rarely drank alcohol, and he never smoked or used illegal drugs, but he had *bad* brain habits like fast food, diet soda, and limited sleep, and he carried unexamined hurts from the past. With changes to his diet and efforts to examine and rectify past hurts, a scan twenty years later proved a younger and healthier brain that had actually aged backward.[1]

Limiting Beliefs under the Surface

Speaking of sand and play, I watched the sun come up over the Atlantic from my time-share condo in Lauderdale-by-the-Sea, a familiar spot where our family roots were planted almost forty years ago. I was digging my toes into the sand with the breeze of the ocean and the constant sounds of large waves hitting the beach with a feeling of intense excitement for a dinner date planned for that evening. There was an unusual insecurity about having this new crush get to know me. I know what you're thinking . . . Penny? Insecure? Yep. I have a few insecurities, and this one was popping up to get my attention.

When my insecurities creep up, they often land in my throat area. They choke me up with emotion when I'm speaking and turn my solid voice into what sounds like a set of twisted bagpipes as I squeak out the message through the emotional lump in my throat. This is a signal I've learned to read about myself that there is something emotional under the surface that deserves some attention. I used to just push it back down and try to swallow the lump, but now I just allow myself to feel my feelings when I'm feeling them, and accept myself as I am. My emotion comes up and out. The wave of emotion is short; then it's gone.

I kind of knew I had an insecurity about meeting this guy, but the previous day when I was meeting my emotional freedom technique (EFT) practitioner Karin Goldgruber by phone, it all became crystal clear. She asked me what I wanted to work on in our session together, and I started by telling her that I honestly had nothing that I felt needed attention. I was having a wonderful solo vacation, things were all good, and I was even super excited to have a date with someone I had recently met whom I was quite smitten with. "I'm just hoping we have a great time because [insert twisted squeaky bagpipe voice here] he's a wealthy gentleman with many great qualities, and I keep thinking that maybe I'm not good enough for him." Boom! There it was, the lump in my throat and the emotion in my voice. . . .

"I guess we know what to work on," Karin stated. The plan for my EFT session was determined.

It wasn't until I spoke the squeaky words that I realized I was insecure about not being good enough for this gentleman . . . but having said that, I really DID always know that I had a lack of confidence at times. I just didn't realize its effect on me. This clue enlightened me to do my inner work, and so I did.

During the EFT tapping session (a practice to relieve emotional stress and pain), Karin had me talk through my emotions about being excited for this guy and this date and the anticipation of what seemed like a new beginning of what could be a beautiful friendship mixed with romance and fun times. I've learned to pay attention to what thoughts and memories come up from my past, because they're clues to understanding my thought patterns and limiting beliefs. While we were working through the first round of tapping, I recalled very vividly a memory of losing my best friend, Janice.

Janice was from a wealthy family. We met in middle school, rode horses together, and spent time at each other's houses for sleepovers and hangouts. Her family and home environment were quite different from mine. We had more people in a much smaller house on a limited budget, and she lived in what I called a mansion, with lots of space and what seemed like an endless supply of money. Her father, VIP they called him, owned a car dealership, and her mom didn't work outside of the home. On weekends, we would go to the barn (equestrian center), and Janice would work with her private coach and ride her expensive horse, and I would rent the schooling horse for the hours that we rode together. The situation worked for me. I was aware of the difference in our families' resources, but at that time I thought I fit right in and worked, played, and acted as if I did. All was blissful and fun.

We were in eighth grade. Our homeroom teacher, Mrs. Thompson, was also our music teacher. I played the trumpet, and Janice played the clarinet. Instrumental music wasn't my favorite subject, and the trumpet didn't come naturally for me, but as a class we played separately and together. All seemed well until the day after parent-teacher night. Janice came to my locker as she always did—we were besties— and she was upset.

"My parents won't allow me to hang around with you anymore." She had tears in her eyes.

"What?" I asked. "Why not?"

"Mrs. Thompson told them you're a bad influence. She told them you are on drugs." She looked embarrassed even to admit what she heard.

"Drugs?" I asked. "What drugs?"

I felt totally angry, falsely accused, betrayed, and victimized. I immediately marched to the office and asked to speak to Mr. Chezni, our principal. I told him what happened and asked to call my dad. When my dad answered the phone, he said he'd be right over to the school to sort this out with me. I was relieved that he had my back.

My father and the principal had words as I sat outside the office. Mrs. Thompson came into their conversation, then left the room, and

5

I was invited back in. Mr. Chezni said that Mrs. Thompson had an apology to make to me personally. I thought everything was going to go back to normal, the lies would be untold, and my friendship with Janice could resume, but there was more.

The betrayal of Mrs. Thompson was never spoken about again. The apology never happened. I believed that adults with authority couldn't be trusted, and the more Janice and I tried to get her parents to reconsider, the more it hurt. Janice told me that her parents wanted her to befriend other girls in our school, and when she named a couple, I realized they were all from wealthy families.

There was more confusion here for me: "Wait . . . what? Your parents don't want me as your friend because of the financial status of our family?" We were a fine family. Double income, decent vehicles, annual vacations. . . . We even worked our butts off at our seasonal business . . . as a family! I made more friends and money the previous summer than Janice had made in her whole life, and I wasn't good enough? Illogical rich people! Absurd, prejudiced idiots! I felt those words, never spoke them, but I pushed them down deep and grew the limiting belief that I'm not good enough for the upper class. That limiting belief is obviously still right under the surface, because it popped out when talking to Karin about my excitement for my date.

Early programming has a long-lasting impact. I'm experiencing the effect of this story at the age of fifty-five, even though it happened over forty years ago. HOLY SHIFT! Time for a change. Had I not been keenly paying attention to my emotional cues, I wouldn't have moved through this.

During my session with Karin, we did some inner healing around not feeling and believing that I am good enough for wealthy people. She used her magical EFT talent to facilitate different conversations, and we used the emotional freedom technique of tapping through them. First, we talked through the insecurity I felt about my current date, and how I'd like it to go. As the session progressed, the deeper issue of losing my best friend popped up, and we simulated a conversation that allowed me to speak my piece to Mrs. Thompson. Karin represented that character in my story, and I spoke to her. We worked through the layers of beliefs that I had made up based on the situation.

We got to a point where she (as Mrs. Thompson) apologized to me. I felt a resistance to receive the apology and move forward. I had been angry for over forty years! That part really stood out for me. I knew that accepting an apology was a tool I needed to play nice in the sandbox . . . but I wasn't willing to pick it up and use it, so we talked about it.

"Why are you so resistant to forgive this teacher who has apologized?" Karin asked.

"It's my old story," I said. "I guess I have to think about why I am so attached to it, who I'll be without it, and what will fill that space in my thinking if I let it go. That sounds like a lot of work that I shouldn't have to do on top of all the pain I've carried since it happened."

But I had a tall, strong, and handsome WHY. He was taking me out for dinner, and I really enjoyed his company and conversation, and with that incentive, I pushed through.

I made a list of a few ways to think differently about it to HOLY SHIFT my perspective. This list came to me quickly. "People of authority aren't perfect and can make mistakes. They are human and need our compassion, empathy, and forgiveness. People of wealthy status won't necessarily betray me. . . . That's new thinking," I admitted to Karin.

I pushed through the walls I had built, even though a part of me wanted to stay stuck in my stance or position of not trusting or being good enough for all people. A strong sense of pride and self-confidence that I had buried filled my heart and my mind, and a brand-new tenderness and vulnerability came over me.

It helps to have a reason to do our work and push through old, limiting beliefs. This gentleman made my heart race. That was enough of a "why" for me, so I decided that for this date I'd just be me without my old story. I'd just be the real authentic Penny. The gal who is who she is, isn't what she isn't, and has what she has. The work I had done to repattern the old thinking created a space for my new behaviors and connections to land.

Doing my inner work to examine and rectify limiting beliefs with mental health practitioners, energy healers, coaches, and meditation over my lifetime has helped me look at my difficult patterns and beliefs. They're so sneaky, but I'm onto them like my own private detective.

There are unconscious things in our current thinking that link backward, and based on the old stories, there might be times when we feel we don't belong, don't fit in, or aren't even invited to play. I hope you can shed some light on them to understand that the assumption is possibly your own thinking that's keeping you on the outside of the community you seek to be part of.

Be willing to leave your old story behind and position yourself well for the opportunities you are seeking. Recognize when you're setting up situations to fail just so you can stay in your old story and complain about it. You have nothing to lose to see what's on the other side of what you're settling for. Be brave and be authentic. There's only one you, so uncover the real raw stuff that prevents you from having what you want.

Self-cultivation is a journey that you move through like layers of an onion. Just when you peel off a layer (which could possibly make you cry), there's another one underneath, and so on. You'll know when something hits you. For me it's tears and/or the twisted, squeaky bagpipes.

What does this personal story have to do with the workplace?

Be More Influential

In my career, I've played within the range that matched my beliefs. If something came across my desk to work with highly paid executives or people of authority with big money, I'd avoid it and make up some reasonable excuse, because I didn't think I'd be a good fit. Since then, I've gone inward to do my self-cultivation. Now I know that I am a good fit, and that the financial status of my clients or circle of friends makes no difference in the skills, capacity, and expertise that I have to empower solid relationships and fair sandbox play.

To bring our best selves to the sandbox of work and life, we need to know what we want, ask for it, and clear the path for it to land. It's that simple, but it's not necessarily that easy. I use my journal to write and reread what I want. It keeps me focused on seeing glimpses in my outer environment of what I am seeking. About two months before I left my hometown for that Florida vacation, I wrote about my future partner and made a list of what he would be like and what I would have to be like to attract someone of his caliber. As that fairy tale continues, three years later, he asked me to marry him, and I said YES!

I encourage audiences to do an "I want" list in a brief partner activity where one person acts as a genie and the other partner tells that genie everything they want. This results in a long list of what the person really wants in their life and workplace. That list is their personal definition of success and can define their direction, align their thoughts, and guide their actions to come out big on the outside, consciously choosing and acting in the direction that's right for them.

Getting clear on what we want helps us take our foot off the brake and uncover limiting beliefs. What are you anticipating and waiting to arrive in your life and career with your foot on the gas full throttle yet an unconscious foot on the brake?

Cultivate What You Want

One of the most liberating concepts I've ever known and taught is that we are all responsible. If you think about the word this way . . . RESPONSE-ABLE . . . being able to choose our response, it helps understand the idea.

If you intend to grow potatoes, you plant potatoes. You intend to yield potatoes in the end, so you cultivate your plants accordingly. The same goes for workplace culture and relationships. If you want a productive, peaceful, and profitable culture, you intend just that and plant those seeds. YOU, not those you work with, are responsible for growing the culture to the best of your ability.

Cultivate means to prepare or work on something, usually relating to growing crops, where there's a tilling of the land required. Tilling is turning over. It's a preparation of the ground to promote growth. So planting potatoes is more than just finding what you want in seed form and planting it, watering it, and tending to it. It's being proactive in preparing the soil.

You are like the soil. Tilling, turning over your thoughts, prepares the groundwork for the fertility of what you want to create. It's the inside work that never ends. Being proactive means to prepare for,

9

intervene in, or control a situation, even a difficult or negative one. When we are proactive, we are in our full power. The opposite is reactive. *React* means to reenact behaviors that are old or habitual. When we react to situations, we are not preparing what we want to happen; rather, we are more like victims of the way they're happening. When we react, we give pieces of our power away, leaving us powerless.

Being proactive is taking the lead in making things happen. We get to stop blaming other people for how things are or are not in our life. Liberating! Because no one but you holds the reins for the cultivation of what you want to grow.

Our Thoughts Shape Our Destiny

Centuries after the classical Newtonian theory that all things were considered solid (matter), and that energy was explained as a force to move objects or change the physical state of matter, Einstein produced the famous $E = mc^2$, demonstrating that energy and matter were one and the same, and completely interchangeable. This set off an exploration of light, which would sometimes behave as wave (energy), and other times as particle (matter), depending on the mind of the observer. From this, the field of science that we know today as quantum physics was born.[2]

At the subatomic level of matter (electrons, protons, neutrons, etc., that make up atoms of all things physical), energy responds to the mind of the observer, and becomes matter. Therefore, **thoughts become things**. The quantum field contains a reality with all elements of your idealized self, whereby using your mind to organize subatomic waves of probability, you can create your desired experiences. To change our lives, we must change the way we think, act, and feel. We must be greater than our current circumstances and environment. When our intentions, behaviors, and actions are equal to our thoughts, our minds and bodies are working together, and this creates immense power behind us.[3] What this really means is that we have the potential to change our personal reality (personality) and create the life we desire. It's law.

Our typical thought pattern is to react, blame, and give our power away.

Why do we react with blame and leave the results in the hands of other people?

Do we think other people have the key to our success?

Do we lack worthiness and a sense of deserving the life we desire?

Do we even know what we desire?

Are we clear on what we want?

We can choose to be proactive and respond differently. We have a great deal of influence on our own journey, but we give so much of it away to other people when we're not taking responsibility for creating what we want.

In the workplace sandbox, we often point the blame outward at other people, policies, or systems that are hurdles in our way. If we envision a pointing hand, one finger points blame elsewhere, but the other three fingers are pointing back at us, because we have much more influence than "they" do. Being influential is empowering. What we CAN do about problems and challenges is far more productive than waiting for someone else to fix or change something so that there are no problems or challenges. This influential thinking works like a muscle. The more you work it, the stronger and bigger it gets, and then we become influential, like Melba did for her whole community in this short story.

I was working in a semiremote First Nation community with a Health Centre team when Melba, the incredibly capable receptionist/secretary/finder of anyone in the office or community, shared some of her biggest and deepest desires for growth. She wanted more skills and training so that she could perform better in her role. She wanted to advance to a higher position and provide a better life for her son. Coaching Melba, I asked her what she was doing about it, and she said that she had asked for some training a while back but hadn't heard anything.

How many times do we stop at one attempt to get what we want or need? We quit way too soon, way too often.

I challenged Melba to inquire on incomplete or unfulfilled requests until she had answers, and I told her about the twelve o'clock method of persistence. This method uses the clock's twelve-hour markings as a symbol for how many times we should follow up on what we're seeking. If we think more of the value in the process of following up with relationship-building efforts, and less on the actual outcome, we'll focus less on emotions (like rejection) and keep on making contact and moving things forward until we either reach the twelfth attempt or have our positive outcome sooner.

Melba accepted my challenge and made a phone call to a training center that same day. Before a month had passed, there was a trainer on-site at her community, giving computer software courses on a regular basis to a committed group of participants. She made more than one contact this time; in fact, she made as many as she had to until successful. She literally championed the entire project by cultivating what she wanted to grow, and in doing so, others grew too.

To provide a better situation for her son, Melba had started some conversations at the school, but no changes were made yet. She used the same strategy of being persistent to follow up on her requests until she gained a better result for her son.

Melba was able to respond differently because I reassured her that she could, and I challenged her to take ownership of what she wanted and stop blaming other people for not paving the way for her. She made it all happen, with just a HOLY SHIFT of her mind, that she could cultivate what she wanted with effort, rather than settling for what others were doing or not doing. She entered her full power.

People like influential people. Influential people make things happen. They get promoted, invited, called to a higher level of sandbox play. To be influential doesn't change the fact that there are concerns and problems and challenges. It means people don't get stuck in them. They move through them. They figure out what to do about the challenges, and they act. Pro-action is the action that we can consciously do, physically or mentally, to move things in the direction we desire. Pro-action is called upon in a crisis that demands an action rather than a debate.

The bottom line is that we are all response-able to create the life we want, and that is liberating. No one can make us feel anything without our permission. No one can really stop us unless we give them that power. No one has power over us unless we give it to them. This is our life. We have the reins to steer it and direct it as we choose.

A sandbox tool to represent cultivation is a hoe. We need to prepare the soil for fertile growth. We need to shift our mindset to one of personal response-ability and perseverance to endure the obstacles that we will face and take ownership to ensure that we are creating the culture that we want for ourselves. Everyone is the leader of their own sandbox of life and work. When we can stand tall in our esteem, our self-worth, and our sense of deserving the very best, we can escape entitlement and feeling that we should be taken care of and shift it to a feeling of "I got this" and "I will make this happen, because I matter, and we matter, and I can empower the result." That is standing in your full power. Rather than being powerless, you will be powerful.

Cultivate what you want to grow. Don't let an unanswered request mean anything other than "It's fertile ground to try again."

Tools for Good Play in a Postpandemic Era

Before you even get to the sandbox, you must gather your tools. Have you ever asked yourself how you're showing up . . . or not showing up to the workplace? Personal inventory for top performance and promotability was the subject of some great interviews with some spectacular human resource managers for their input on the question. **What qualities or characteristics are you looking for in a new hire, or for promotability into higher- or senior-level positions?**

In a *Harvard Business Review* interview with Lauren Smith, VP at Gartner Research, reengineering the recruitment process to rebuild and adapt to a virtual or hybrid environment has shifted the landscape for organizations' hiring and internal promotion process.[4] Many organizations can now recruit talent outside of their geographical region, as they seek to build the workforce of the future and not just replace the former one. This is an opportunity to advance their diversity and to open promotions to internal candidates who are self-taught, regardless of meeting educational requirements.

Hiring and HR managers are seeking potential over credentials, suggesting that a great candidate can grow with their organization over time. Potential is determined by things like curiosity, agility, and teamwork.[5]

Curiosity helps us develop emotionally, mentally, intellectually, and even physically, through knowledge attainment.[6] Being curious helps us evolve as a human, increases workplace success, expands empathy, reduces stress, and benefits those around us.[7] Asking why and using deeper questions to understand others create emotional interactions and meaningful conversations that build experiences together, which builds connection, which builds success.

Agility is the ability to make progress amid the modern demands and ever-changing workplace landscape. A team member who is agile in their thinking and skill set is an asset because they are more fluid than "set in stone" to adapt where new roles, business demands, and work environments are changing.[8] (We never use cement in a sandbox, right?)

Teamwork has changed considerably in the COVID-19 landscape. Although 90 percent of companies felt their culture improved with remote work,[9] people are expecting the same employee experience (EX) of working together in highly collaborative ways. Individual team working skills required to succeed in today's hybrid working environment are active listening and empathy,[10] which we will cover in later chapters of this book.

Curiosity, agility, and teamwork help people manage relationships or improve career potential with their "sandbox factor." How people conduct themselves and manage their workplace relationships matters because their sandbox factor is taken into consideration as a great candidate for promotions and hiring. Their overall fit is not just measured by their technical training or expertise. To fit with a team, organizations need people who breed healthy culture; have people skills; and can problem solve, adapt with change, anticipate interpersonal conflicts, and have courageous conversations to mitigate or resolve them.

Some of the biggest challenges HR managers shared with me during interviews before the pandemic were a lack of understanding and disagreements that stem from someone's tunnel vision, rather than a broad view of the overall organizational goals. I interviewed three HR managers from three different sectors to inquire about the characteristics they look for in hiring and promotion decisions. They told me that they look for people who:

- Have insight into themselves (seek to understand themselves)
- Are resilient
- Work toward mastering their emotional intelligence
- Can respond versus react to situations, especially unexpected ones
- Are humble enough to admit their mistakes, apologize, and restore relationships that have been shaken
- Seek to understand others, have empathy and compassion
- Can detach from their personal opinions to fit in with a team

A common mention was a desire to have team members who didn't provoke or intensify heightened situations—rather, could "keep calm and move through the sandstorm." Knowing how to respond and choosing that, rather than reacting to the emotions felt at the time, is a skill. It's difficult to be appropriate in all situations because we're human, and emotions act faster than logic in our brains, so as easy as this sounds, we don't always do well at playing nice when the going gets tough.

I always remind people that communication is an art, not a science. It will never be perfect, and we can always be honest, apologize, and try again until things feel and sound better. During a management meeting, Laura, a department manager, was asked to speak to some progress she was accountable for. In doing so, she pointed the blame at Tom, another department manager (referred to as "throwing someone under the bus"). This lack of responsibility and blame was done in front of Tom's boss and the CEO, and created personality conflict issues on top of the issues Laura was accountable for in the first place. Not only did Laura make an impression on management at the meeting that she had a low sandbox factor, but the tension also trickled into their respective departments.

> Meeting chair: "Laura, did your sales department work harder to reach our projected target for widgets this quarter?"
> Laura: "I would like to report a sales increase; however, the quality of the widgets was substandard for market, and I asked Tom to deal with it at his department, but I never heard back."
> Tom: "You can't pin your poor sales and unproductive team on me."

Result: The whole room feels awkward. . . . Conflict brews between Laura and Tom.

Even when he's out from under the bus, Tom will always remember how this situation made him feel, and so will the other colleagues at the table, including HR. There are more subtle ways to gain people's support, although the inappropriate ways are often remembered.

It's never too late to plant the seeds of the harvest you want. In the case of Laura and Tom, there were common mistakes made. We are all human. No one is perfect, so we sometimes (some more often than others) can come off harsh or abrasive, but we always have an important tool at our disposal. It's the apology tool. Like the old Etch-a-Sketch toy that you could just shake your drawing and it would disappear. If you can recall a time when you passed the buck or pointed the blame elsewhere instead of taking responsibility, then you can always go back and untangle the knot with a sincere apology and clean the situation up.

People will always remember how you made them feel.

I've learned that people will forget what you said, people will forget what you did, but people will never forget how you made them feel.
—Maya Angelou

"Is a sandbox factor more valuable than technical training and experience?" I asked the dynamic HR manager of a hospital to share some personal experiences with me. He asked me if I wanted a story of how one's sandbox factor helped them rise, or one about how a lack of sandbox factor held someone back.

"Both, of course," I said. "Why would I settle for half of this gift?"

Let's Compare High/Low Sandbox Factor

Brent, a bachelor of commerce grad in finance and newly minted certified professional accountant (CPA), was newly hired into management. One of the youngest managers in training, he was given the opportunity based on minimal credentials of management experience and on a trial basis to prove himself. He had the technical background and a goal to develop into the subtleties that make a good manager. Shortly after starting, Brent was well liked. He was fair, consistent, and someone the staff could go to for assistance with problem solving. He had the ability to do his own job and to bring people together to be more effective than they could be on their own. He was open minded to learn from the person he just hired, or the person who was retiring. "Everyone has something to teach you, something to tell you, or something to add," he'd say.

A good leader creates other leaders, as opposed to just creating followers. Brent's ability to empower others contributed greatly to the team's productivity and function. Just as success breeds success, his responsibility grew rapidly, his salary grew to match his contribution, and things moved along in an incline with career advancement, because he was always recognized by senior managers as adding great value. Looking back at the trajectory of his career, his sandbox factor got him a great distance, comparable with his other accountant colleagues who haven't been given promotions. Brett's likability set him apart from others—people skills are very important to support technical skills. There are many accountants, but how many technical expertise people have an open mind to learn from the team around them? Brent shot for the stars and developed those additional people skills, which brought him over the top.

Let's compare that career progress to Kurt's. Kurt was remembered by my HR interviewee while working in a casino's talent acquisition department. The turnover was rapid, and they needed more managers and supervisors. Kurt, an exceptional card dealer who was impeccable with his skill, was so technically versed in his job that he could calculate the odds of betting at 35:1 ratio in his head. He was completely knowledgeable about everything in every game he dealt, except the game of collaboration and teamwork. He had applied several times for a supervisory opportunity, described as a position to guide and help the other dealers, figure out payments, deal with customer service issues, and assist with employee development. Every time he applied, he was passed over by management. He was constantly denied. My HR interviewee wondered how they could pass this guy up. He was the highest rated in his initial position as a dealer, earning the highest salary, but he couldn't advance beyond that.

After meeting with the decision-makers, it was presumed that Kurt wouldn't help others and he wouldn't build up the employees coming up around him, because he had a self-centered, arrogant approach to his work, and he wasn't willing to help his teammates grow into his caliber of service delivery as a dealer. He felt that because he learned everything himself, others should too. He was more concerned with *being the best*, rather than developing the best team of people. In Kurt's mind, you don't lift people up, you step on them while they're trying to rise to the occasion of growth, and in doing so Kurt got back exactly that: a stunted career.

Situations and past dealings with people can follow us professionally, whether they're written on a personnel file or not. The effects of how we *make people feel* are worth considering. People have choices to stay with an organization or leave. Good people are worth keeping, and sometimes you will see people leapfrog over others along their career journey because they have developed their ability to empower other people to perform at their personal best. I believe that if we take responsibility for our own lives, no one can make us feel anything without our permission; however, people can influence us to want to follow them or not, and that's what leaders need to be cognizant of today.

Poor sandbox performance can lead to letters on someone's human resources file and usually occur when complaints are made formal and/ or when investigations are required, but there are also the unwritten experiences that decision-makers remember about who is ready for managing people and who isn't.

Most often, we're not focusing on relationship management because we're focused on results management, and we're doing so at the cost of relationships. What if we could focus on both relationships and results?

In a sandstorm, don't jump to the point of a formal complaint or investigation. Use your tools. Cultivate what you want to grow, invite people to talk about it, ask for help when you need it, apologize when you know you haven't done the right thing, and be patient with yourself. "Per-fekt" your sandbox play. . . . *Perfect* being a verb, because you will never be *perfect* (adjective), and neither will anyone else.

"Know thyself," an ancient Greek aphorism from Socrates, the moral and ethical philosopher, has meanings that vary among his students, most pointing to the idea of continuous self-discovery, self-reflection, and self-referencing.[11] Fast-forward to today, the inward reflection of ourselves will build a solid foundation for our own greatest castle. Self-cultivation is not a destination, but a journey worth exploring. The clearer we are about what we want in our lives, and the more confident we are that thoughts become things, the better we become at influencing others who want to follow. To be proactive, we take responsibility for creating the life we want to live, and because so much of conflict resolution is an inside job, investing in our sandbox factor will provide immeasurable results, because relationships are at the root of all human success.

Have you found a valuable nugget or opportunity in this chapter that you'd like to implement? This is an opportunity for a HOLY SHIFT in your mindset and behavior. Write it down where you will see it often or download our worksheet companion.

The tools for good play, performance, and promotions begin with positioning yourself inward first to do your internal, personal leadership development. But wait . . . these tools are bulky, and you only have so much internal space! Are you willing to declutter and unpack some of your old stuff? Let's see if you're willing even to look at old baggage that's weighing you down and unpack it so that you have room for your new inventory of tools to *PLAY NICE*.

Lighten Your Load

Unpack to make space for new relationship tools.

IS YOUR PAST NAVIGATING YOUR FUTURE?

Imagine dragging a large suitcase along with you wherever you go. It's chock full of past experiences, which can both help you through your day-to-day interactions, decisions, and tasks, *and* hinder you from showing up in your full power and present-moment thinking. Unresolved conflicts or self-deprecating meanings to old stories can get in the way of how you deal with current-moment situations. Living from the confines of our old baggage can cause unnecessary problems. Can you imagine how inaccurate assumptions about current circumstances could take place? Many people have no idea that they're packing around stuff that limits them from living a fully authentic and free life, and most of it is unnecessary, tiresome, limiting, and optional. You can choose to unpack the unwanted and make room for better tools.

The brain is the starting point of our thoughts and feelings. Neuroscientific theory states that our brain is organized to reflect all that we know, from knowledge and past experiences, stored in our synaptic connections.[1] Synapses are the functional connection between neurons, which are necessary for the transfer of electric activity or chemical activity from one cell to another.[2] The people, places, times, experiences are all configured within the structure of our brains; additionally, the behaviors and actions that we've performed and mastered are all recorded as reflection "memories" of our personal past. When we think from these past memories of our mind, we remind (re-mind) ourselves of who we think we are, and therefore create more of the same.[3] Hebb's law states that "nerve cells that fire together, wire together," meaning that by repeatedly activating the same thoughts, the neurons develop long-term relationships.[4] Often referred to as "hardwired," these long-lasting connections of thoughts and behaviors become patterns, automatic and unconscious habits of thinking.

What's in Your Suitcase?

It's likely that our ability to play in a workplace sandbox is being driven by experiences from the past. We unconsciously tap into thought patterns and pathways to respond to current situations, make decisions, or interact with others. This is where we get into trouble or limit our potential, because not only are we using old thinking to understand, create meaning, and solve new problems, but we're also unable to create change in the pattern, so we live on a hypothetical hamster wheel, and keep re-creating the same outcome.

When we show up to situations, we bring the inventory of our past and our connection to it. I refer to the old hardwiring of past experiences, meanings, and stories we've made up about it all as baggage that we carry around in our "suitcase," and many of these stories are fiction. The collection of these stories becomes larger with age, each one having effects on the way we think, feel, and as a result . . . behave. This creates an inner conflict, because even though we may know better, we don't always feel better or do better. There are external conflicts created with other people as well because everyone has a suitcase, and therefore, interpersonal relationships get complicated because there are times when our stories get entangled with someone else's stories. Clash! We have conflict stemming from old stuff that we often don't even understand of our own, plus the baggage that belongs to someone else that we or they don't understand either.

Several years ago, I was working with a speaking coach who made me aware that when I stand in front of an audience, I am bringing everything with me from my past. What??? I was horrified to think that when I show up as a trainer or speaker in front of an audience who is there to learn how to *PLAY NICE* in the sandbox, I am bringing old baggage with me, and they can somehow *tell* that I have baggage! OMG, that was enough to motivate me to figure this out. I took some time to envision what might be in my suitcase, especially the items that I might want to unpack, like unresolved conflict, resentment, and fear. Not only did I want to figure out what's inside, and how it may have got there, but more importantly, how do I get rid of what I know is weighing me down? And so I began to dig in and was shocked and amazed at the long list of stuff. That's a lot of baggage to be carrying around.

I've learned over the years as an expert in workplace relationships that everyone has a similar suitcase of their own stuff. Since I recognize how the attachment to my past creates my future, I've been able to detach from it, find peace, and create something new. It's a work in progress because old patterns die hard. I've also been able to help thousands of people do the same. Let me share one of the "stories" that came up for me and how I worked through it.

As I graduated from high school and was applying for postsecondary education, there was a conflict between my dad and me. He wanted me to be a court reporter or a secretary, but I wanted to be a fashion model. Conflict!

I agreed to apply to be a court reporter by writing a test at a school in Toronto. We packed the car and drove to the big city together. It was a great father-daughter getaway. He invested quite a bit of time, money, and effort into our trip. The day after we arrived, I wrote the aptitude test for the court reporting school with an honest effort. A few weeks later, a letter from the college arrived. When I opened it in front of him and read the rejection out loud, my heart sank, and my dad yelled, "YOU'RE TOO STUPID TO GO TO COLLEGE!" He was very disappointed, and I was hurt by his reaction.

I didn't want to believe that I wasn't smart enough to go to college, but somewhere in the deep, dark depths of my emotional programming . . . it stuck and I chose to carry it around with me, even though I didn't want to be a court reporter anyway. By the way, I got my wish. I was a fashion model in Toronto . . . for about two weeks. The other models and agents were unfriendly, envious, and cranky, which was not a match to my northern girl sandbox style, so I kept looking for work in the big city to fund my life. I landed a job in the business district of Toronto and was so excited to call my mom and dad with the great news that I was officially . . . a secretary.

Even though I ended up being what my dad wanted me to be, I still chose to unconsciously carry around the limiting belief that "I'm not smart enough" at best, and "I'm too stupid" at worst. Unfortunately, the story held me back for about thirty years, because I didn't even realize that it was an unnecessary tool in my tool kit. My unconscious story of "I'm not smart enough" hadn't surfaced yet in my conscious mind, but it sure was navigating my future.

My attachment to that story kept me from having the courage to go to postsecondary education and from achieving my own best results, because I had limiting beliefs about my potential. When I did pursue new things and they became difficult, I'd check out and curl up into the comfortable place to hide in my old story that "I'm not good enough, or I'm too stupid." Even when I was a secretary and doing well, advancing with skills and job promotions, I would run into hurdles, and I'd instantly go from being a middle-aged professional to a sixteen-year-old college reject. Once I realized that the attachment to my past kept re-creating my future, I committed to detaching from it, and I knew that the work I had to do was an inside job.

I had never forgotten the day I opened the rejection letter and heard his harsh words. I was able to forgive him shortly after it happened, but I did harbor resentment, which took the form of rebellion. I'd show him. I'll be the opposite of his opinion, and that became my default . . . accomplishments rooted in unconscious rebellion. I did well as a young adult, I started my own business, had a beautiful family, and maintained good relationships with my parents as I went through the stages of being both a parent and a professional, but once I became aware that my old story was lingering under the surface of a new level of success, I knew I needed a HOLY SHIFT.

To create the shift in my old thinking, I made a list in my journal of all the things I am good at and have been good at. I listed great mom, daughter, friend, and entrepreneur; studied mediation and complex disputes at Harvard; and helped thousands of people build productive, peaceful, and profitable relationships at work and in business. Most importantly, I commended myself for forgiving my father shortly after his harsh words.

Thank goodness I decided to forgive him as a teenager, because when I put myself in his shoes, I realized that he was stressed and imperfect and had made a few mistakes as a parent. I'm also an imperfect parent, trying to juggle the demands of work and life, and sometimes I say the wrong things and hurt my kids' feelings. It's unintentional, but it happens. Looking back, I am grateful that I didn't waste decades being disconnected or estranged from him. But I didn't really resolve the effects of those words until later in life, when I did the work of rewriting the story in my mind. It was only then that I really chose to let it go and found peace.

The inner work required to work through this one was all mine to do. Had my father been alive, I may have had the conversation with him so that we could work through what happened and how it affected me, but he had passed away a few years before, and as close as we were when he was alive, we were no longer able to connect in the physical form. I had my conversations with him in the spirit world. I used my journal and prayer to work through my own healing. I felt his immediate response. It was one of love, empowerment, and reassurance that I am enough, I am loved, and I can have whatever I want. Most importantly, I took the responsibility needed to make it right for me, and I shed the weight of that story from my suitcase, which has made room, space, and potential for better tools. The momentum from clearing this inspired me to clear more, and to dig, and to reap the benefits over and over again of resolving old conflicts to peace.

Our past will always be our past, but our connection to it can be very different. Rather than being attached to the limiting beliefs created in my early emotional programming, I've learned the value of detaching from those old stories and writing new ones. The awareness that these old stories forged the original and easiest thought pathways is demonstrated time and time again when things get tough and my "I'm too stupid" story gets triggered; but now I have new awareness to recognize those times and to get attached to something more productive toward my potential. Mastering our own emotions is an inside job, and an ongoing process that gets easier over time.

We all have a suitcase, and being aware of its contents helps us understand ourselves at a greater depth. Wouldn't it be great if we all had a bright flashlight to shine down into ourselves and see everything that we're carrying around? Or if someone invented an X-ray machine to see through our emotional baggage?

You become aware of stuff in your suitcase that doesn't serve you by the conflict that it arouses, so learn to embrace that conflict. Be grateful for what it's showing you. In your personal or career adult lives, there are times when you'll be triggered emotionally by conflict that has a significant attachment to your past. The interesting thing is that unless you are fully aware of the old stuff that you're carrying around in your suitcase, you may only be seeing the tip of the iceberg, while the portion under the surface is very important to understand. Once you understand a circumstance, you're in a great position to deal with it. Knowing where feelings are coming from, why you think the way you think and behave the way you behave, is the first step to shifting it.

Why We're So Attached to Our "Stuff"

Has an interaction with someone ever left you feeling stupid or not enough? I'll bet your first instinct is to blame the other person, but let's face it, if they've pushed a button in you, then you can take responsibility for even having that button for them to push. Finding peace begins with awareness.

Part of unpacking your suitcase is not just knowing what's in it, but also why you're so attached to the old thinking. What's the payoff for staying attached to it?

A bright light of awareness can allow all kinds of junk to be found in our suitcase of old stuff. If you want to see what's in your suitcase, you will start to connect the dots, find the linkage from how the stories of the past can keep you on that hamster wheel. I'll warn you now, once you see these things, you'll never unsee them. You can turn the lights off, but you'll never unsee the truth, and that's a good thing.

Some people want to stop there, just seeing what's inside, because they've been conditioned to avoid the conflict of difficult conversations. I encourage you to keep digging! These stories are navigating your future, and either you're conscious of them or you're not. Don't you want to be steering your own ship? Detaching from old thought patterns is easier when you understand why you continue to think them. Here are several reasons why people are so attached to their stuff.

Old Programming/Wiring

As mentioned earlier, our emotional programming begins at an early age and creates pathways for thought. The nerve cells of the brain (neurons) have single elongated extensions (axons) that send messages. When two messages "connect," the axons join forming a synapse, like a bridge or connection. They get wired together and are used for memory and recollection. This "hardwiring" is not always relevant or accurate for current use.

Think about how we can be wiring up thought patterns that create our own limiting beliefs, like "I'm stupid when it comes to writing tests" or "I'm not good enough for wealthy people." Those are just two of what could be countless ways of misinterpreting messages from old wiring.

Programming can be inherited from our lineage: biological parents, grandparents, even spouses and ex-lovers.[5] The unconscious mind doesn't differentiate between what's present moment and what it remembers from the past, so in current time we can often be speaking and listening through this old wiring. Do you see then how we could go from a fifty-year-old professional woman to a sixteen-year-old college reject in a snap?

Fear of Conflict and Difficult Conversations

Another reason we've become so attached to our old stories and thought patterns is that we're uncomfortable with conversations that are confrontational, challenging, or negative. We think it's easier to avoid them than to gather the people involved and talk about it, so we harbor the resentment or gossip/vent to the wrong people instead of taking the road less traveled. We're attached to comfort and perceive conflict and conversations as difficult, but our comfort zone really isn't all that comfortable, is it?

Fight-or-Flight Hormones

We have stress hormones built into our DNA to fight, take flight, or freeze. Those were important back in the day when a saber-toothed tiger would have popped out of the bush and threatened to eat us, but the reality is that today we don't have to choose fight-or-flight, and instead we use these hormones by exaggerating minor stressful situations into major catastrophes. We make mountains out of molehills. This allows our innate hormones to be useful, and we feel satisfied with our own ability to protect ourselves. The ego's job is to protect us, so when we give it something to protect us from, we are actually stroking our ego for doing a good job, protecting us from mountains that really could just be molehills.

Reasonable Excuses

Excuses that sound reasonable to us are still excuses. And the ones we make up to hold on to old stuff are plentiful. Excuses like "I'm too busy," "I'm just not that kind of person," or "I'm Irish" are all just excuses, and they could be holding you back from a whole other level of connection, unless you're onto yourself about how you're holding yourself back. Of course, the excuses seem easier than doing the deeper work, but anything worth having is worth doing the work.

Emotional Addiction

When those networks of neurons are fired in our brain, it creates electrical charges. Those thoughts can also cause a chemical reaction that results in a feeling or emotion.[6] Emotions are chemical feedback, an end product of our experiences. If you've spent years thinking and feeling a certain way that triggers an emotion and chemical reaction, you've conditioned your body to become addicted to the emotions.[7]

Remember the stuff I found in my suitcase about my dad telling me I was too stupid to go to college? I had no idea that I was unconsciously so attached to that story. I knew I was totally upset, insulted, and feeling verbally abused in that circumstance. Perhaps I was making a mountain out of a molehill, but I didn't realize I was using it as a place to curl up and hide from many challenges thereafter and using the old story as a reasonable excuse to check out when the going got tough until many years later. Once I became aware of it was I onto myself like a private detective solving a puzzle; I started uncovering the patterns of thought that were old and limiting.

Some of the questions I ask when digging to find where behavior patterns come from are:

What's your earliest recollection of this happening in your life?
What's under this?
What are you getting out of it?

There's often something deeper than what we see on the surface, and our behavior is usually motivated by old thinking. Dig deep and see what you can uncover. Some of the greatest gifts of life are wrapped up in awful giftwrap. Unpack them with curiosity to polish up the content of those stories and turn them into gems! There is tremendous value in adversity when we're willing to explore and mine for the treasure that can help us grow.

Linking this story to my work sandbox, I've had to learn to accept feedback. When I first hear or read feedback about my work, I see it through my "I'm not good enough" eyes, but being aware of my default thought patterns, I can put on my big-girl pants and see it for what it is: an opportunity to find a HOLY SHIFT in perspective.

You'll know when something is in your suitcase when it continues to be entangled in conflict that agitates you. Whether big or small symptoms occur, they're just feedback that there's something to deal with, smooth over, or let go. Dig in and unpack that stuff. Reflect on it to ensure that you're seeing it from all angles, including "why" you're so attached to it.

Whether it is old wiring, fear of difficult conversations or conflict, your ego protection, some reasonable excuse, or an emotional addiction, you can get to the bottom of why you're attached to your old story and truly understand the bigger picture of who you are. There's a fine line between ego protection and doing what's best. When we are clear on why we're so attached our old stories, we can start to contemplate who we could be without them. Now, that is an amazing reason to get excited about detaching from the old stuff. Or . . . maybe it's another reason to stay attached, depending on your willingness to move forward.

What do you think your reasons are for staying attached to some of your old stories? Write them down as opportunities to HOLY SHIFT for self-development! I hope you're inspired to shine the light within, not fearful of what you'll find, because I guarantee you that knowing who you are and what's navigating your future is far more beneficial than carrying around unnecessary obstacles to the relationships you're seeking.

What's on the other side of detaching from old baggage is empty space, like a blank canvas, and there's just so much freedom to create whatever you want when you're working with an empty space or blank canvas. Here are some options to unpack and lighten your load.

Unpack and Let Go

You know you're packing around stuff, you've got some good ideas on why you're so attached to that stuff, and hopefully you're ready to unpack it, detach, and let it go! Here are some ideas on how to do that.

Your past will always be your past, but you can change your **attachment** to it, which can shift it from a liability to an asset. This is great news, because you get to decide how you want your past to affect your present and future. There's a price to pay for carrying around old baggage, and there's a price to pay for lightening your load, so the real question is, what result do you want?

Pay Attention to Your Feelings

To lighten your load and unpack your suitcase, pay attention to your feelings. They're a guidance system offering constant feedback. Feelings like *frustration, anger, depression, fear, despair, powerlessness, grief, insecurity, guilt, unworthiness, jealousy, hatred, rage, revenge, discouragement, blame, worry, doubt, disappointment, overwhelm, irritation, impatience, pessimism, boredom (are you feeling awful yet?)* are a good indication that you might find a connection to some stored emotion from your past.

Sit quietly and ask yourself where this feeling is coming from. Listen (pay attention) to the answers that enter your mind; then try to trace back to earlier situations and circumstances where similar thoughts and thinking were created. Those earliest memories hold a lot of healing potential.

Unpack to Your Journal

Make a written record of what you're experiencing conflict with. Notice patterns of behavior or thinking. I recommend a journal to everyone I teach, speak to, or coach, because there is magic that happens when we write on paper. The flow of thoughts, the feelings put to words, and the venting or dumping of ideas helps us rid ourselves of the burdens and see the misinformation that's spinning in our mind. Life is so busy that it's difficult to be living it and contemplating the how and why we're living it at the same time, so I use paper to remember, and also to forget.

Write about what's on your mind and where it comes from by thinking about the earliest time in your life when you can recall a similar thought or a related experience. That is digging into what is underneath the current conflict and helps you connect dots and associate old patterns of thinking with real-time circumstances. Also write about your strengths and gather evidence against your old stories. The written personal testimonies of your successes will help you choose to attach to your potential.

Writing, poetry, stories, or scrapbooking are all methods used to explore. Defined as journaling, the process helps gain insights and get in touch with one's feelings by reflecting and analyzing life, events, and people. By writing experiences, reflections, and the personal meaning assigned to them, there is an interplay between the conscious and unconscious that occurs.[8] Journaling is holistic in its approach to therapy because it involves the physical (movement), mental (processing thoughts), emotional (expression of feelings), and spiritual (finding meaning). By identifying unconscious emotions and ideas that could be influencing behaviors, you can link them with past or future implications. Journaling provides an avenue to become more self-reliant by developing inner strength and can provide an opportunity to socially reconstruct past psychological injury.[9]

The process of journaling often outweighs its content.[10] Its intention is to produce private and introspective content, unless you want it to be shared. Be honest with yourself and your true feelings. Over the years I have used many types of journals, diaries, fancy books, or digital media, but my favorite is the old-fashioned three-ring binder with lined paper because things can be easily moved around to be read often or never again, and no one has ever taken my binder off the bookshelf to read it because it does not resemble a diary.

Unpack with Meditation

There's a concept that we have three brains that allow us to move from thinking—to doing—to being. Even better is the idea that when you focus your attention to exclude your environment, body, and time, you can easily move from thinking to being, without having to "do" anything. Your brain doesn't distinguish between what is happening in the outer world (reality) and what is happening in the inner reality of your mind; therefore, if you can mentally rehearse a desired experience in thought alone and the emotions of the event before it has physically manifested, you are already moving into the state of being because your mind and body are in coherence (working as one). You can rewrite your habits, attitudes, and unwanted subconscious programs.[11] I am a student of Dr. Joe Dispenza,[12] author of books on the science and techniques to create a new mind and become supernatural through meditation. These guided meditations continue to help me break old patterns and create new ones. Daily practice of meditation is well worth the investment of time.

Unpack with Professional Help

A lot of people are afraid, ashamed, or embarrassed to talk about mental health issues, but most people will experience a mental health issue at some point in their lifetime.[13] Many workplaces have an employee assistance program (EAP) or benefits that assist with the cost of a counselor. These are confidential opportunities to talk to someone who is licensed and trained to assist with mental health. There are other options for professional mental health service providers available to us. Tap into them and become the best version of yourself with professional guidance. We must destigmatize the use of mental health professionals and encourage wellness of the physical, mental, emotional, and spiritual self. Talk to someone, and don't be shy to promote the benefits of counseling. My personal use of a psychologist at least twice a year through my benefit plan has given me incredible guidance. Several of my good friends are psychotherapists, and I reach out to them often. It frightens me to think who I'd be today without the professional help that has helped me through conflict.

Unpack with Conversations

When we can sit with people we feel resentment toward and have conversations about how we've been affected, how we're feeling, or how much about ourselves and our own entanglement in the situation we've come to understand, we can begin to unravel, unpack, and unlock old items from our past that give us new space to grow. Seeking to understand our own issues, where they come from, or who has planted them within us, along with the realization of when (how long ago) it arrived in our psyche, can really help us become ready to move through the healing.

Don't be afraid to approach difficult conversations. The only way through conflict is through it. You can't go over it, under it, or around it. You can only reach the other side of conflict by confronting (eloquently) the issues in front of you. With some training and practice, you can work through issues with face-to-face conversation with the people involved. This is an art that we must keep alive, the ability to connect and communicate our truth, be understood, and reciprocate understanding to others.

Turn Stumbling Blocks into Humbling Blocks

Although our ego's job is to protect us, overprotecting ourselves by being stubborn, resistant, or refusing to embrace conflict that continues to surface is a stumbling block that can be overcome by being aware and motivated to do the work to make peace and let it go. Recovering requires self-awareness, self-reflection, recognizing why you're attached to your stuff, and the courage to clean it up and let it go. You'll be personally developing, practicing good communication skills, and creating better relationships with yourself and others. The issues causing conflict really aren't stumbling blocks, then; they're humbling blocks.

In Anishinaabe tradition, there are Seven Grandfather Teachings[14] for principles of character that each should live by: Love, Respect, Bravery, Truth, Honesty, Wisdom, and Humility. Each is represented by an animal. Humility is represented by the wolf that lives life for and within the pack. Humility teaches us to find a balance within ourselves because all beings are equal.[15] We are not above nor beneath anyone. Community is very important to humans as well, and leaders with humility can improve team performance and viability.[16]

Communication through difficult times is an act of humility, and an art that society is losing. Texting and digital communication that is not real time, face-to-face, is changing the way people connect, but it's too easy to hide behind a keypad and say what's on your mind. Anything in the "difficult conversation" zone should be shared face-to-face, by video chat, or at least by phone conversation, leaving less chance for misinterpretation and more chance for compassion, empathy, and human connection.

Unpack Early . . . How about Today?

The most stressful part of being in conflict or building up to a challenging conversation is right before you talk about it, but talking about it is less stressful than spinning in it, because your mind can spiral off on many trails of thought that evoke emotions, based on fear.

Fear is most often just false experiences appearing real (FEAR).

It takes a lot of energy to conjure up all those fear-based guesses of what the real issues even are, so until you get talking about it (with the right person[s]), you're spinning and stressed. The best person to talk about it with is the person who you're having conflict with. If you don't feel safe or prepared to do that, reach out to a trusted professional, HR manager, or someone who will help you develop a plan of action.

Invite the other party to the conversation. "Can we talk?" is the easiest approach. Your goal is to get them to the conversation, so choose friendly words and an inviting voice tone. I used to say, "We need to talk" . . . and it got me nowhere. Simple as well, but it sounded more like an order than an invitation. Here are some other options:

"I have an idea that I think will help us work together more
   effectively."
"I'd like to talk about _____ with you to get your point of
   view."
"Do you have a few minutes to chat? I need your help with what
   just happened."
"I think we have different perspectives on _____ and I'd like to
   hear your thoughts on this."
"Would you agree to talk with me about _____ until we find
   a solution that we both feel good about?"

When you do get the chance to talk, try to listen and speak (in that order if possible) from the present, not the past.

Unpack with Time

I've witnessed the unpacking of old stories merely in the awareness of their existence, and a recognition that there has been a considerable amount of time between old stories and present-moment happenings, and that to solve present problems, we shouldn't be using old thought patterns. This does not mean sweeping issues under the carpet, or "letting go" because of time if you really don't feel peace about a situation.

While doing a two-day workplace restoration circle with a Health Centre team, I noticed a quiet woman, Deanna, listening and attentive, but not speaking up. On the second day, she arrived with such enthusiasm to share the results of her homework. When Deanna was seven years old, her father, one of her most trusted protectors and teachers, quickly tapped her mouth with the back of his fingers to shush her. Deanna couldn't remember why or what she had said or any of the details, other than . . . from that day forward, she stopped talking.

When Deanna came to understand what she was packing around all these years in her suitcase that was preventing her from speaking up, her transformation was instant. She realized she was speaking and listening from a seven-year-old perspective, but she was forty-nine! Just in the realization, the unpacking of what was holding her back, she stepped into present-time thinking with a renewed perspective. Within a few weeks, Deanna applied for and was promoted to the organization's general manager position, which extended far beyond her department, to lead a team of several departments.

Letting go of the attachment of past programming and wounds helps us make space to attach to our potential. When you start letting go of the smaller things in your suitcase, you build momentum and space for other things you'd rather carry with you, like faith, hope, courage, love, passion, energy, enthusiasm, forgiveness, time, kindness, grace, generosity, conversation, acceptance . . . there is so much potential for good tools.

Our suitcase of tools for best workplace sandbox interactions can be unpacked and repacked with the tools that will serve us. Old programming, old thinking, old patterns, reasonable excuses, and emotional addictions aren't going to help us grow in the present time. We can make room in our suitcase by weeding out the items that aren't useful and replacing them with tools and inventory that are. Start by unpacking the smaller things and use the extra space and momentum inside you to tackle the bigger ones.

With all this information about the potential contents of your suitcase, take a few moments to take inventory of those old stories or limiting beliefs that are creating inner or outer conflict in your life and workplace. Ask yourself what you would find in your suitcase if you took an honest look, or if you asked to see what you needed to see. This is an opportunity for a HOLY SHIFT of your mindset and behavior. Write it down where you will remember to take action on unpacking these stories. Consider using our HOLY SHIFT downloadable worksheet companion.

Pick an item that you want to unpack; then chose a method to break those old, hardwired beliefs. You can journal, meditate, have conversations to find resolution, seek professional help, or all the above.

Be grateful for the conflict that surfaces when looking into your past or as it arises daily because there are lessons to learn in the entanglements with others. The payoff of having difficult conversations with humility and courage far outweigh the fear of having them.

Life isn't just about feeling good all the time—it's about doing what's right. Short-term discomfort toward something worth having is well worth the investment of time, vulnerability, and effort. It's possible all you'll gain is the knowledge that you really tried your absolute best, and there is peace in that resolution itself.

Now is the best time to make peace with your past so it doesn't mess up your future, for although your past might be a great teacher, it's a terrible master.

3

Actively Listen

Help others feel understood.

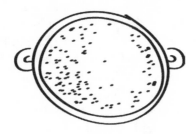

Do you listen with the intention to respond, or do you listen with the intention to understand?

Listening can build rapport, dissolve conflict, and get better results at anything relationship based, which is . . . most things ☺.

To actively listen is like using a sand sifter. A little person would hold on to a sand sifter with both hands because sand is heavy, which is symbolic to giving our full attention and not multitasking. Also symbolic to a sifter, as sand (words) come in, only the facts would filter through, leaving the judgments, analysis, and advice caught in the sifter. This simple concept is not so easy to master.

It sounds easier than it is. You might be thinking, "Yeah I listen all the time," but do you really *actively listen?* There's a difference. I explain it like this: Seeing is to reading like hearing is to listening. Just because you are seeing something, doesn't mean you're reading it with comprehension. Just because you're hearing someone, giving them time to talk while you're taking a pause from talking, doesn't mean you're comprehending what they're saying. The difference in actively listening is in taking the action to communicate back what you've heard.

The art of active listening takes awareness and practice. What often gets in the way is the habit of having a conversation much like a ping-pong game, where the topic bounces back and forth between people, back and forth with comments. There are two people talking, but no one's actively listening.

Consider emotionally charged conversations, where active listening is more challenged because the right side of our brain reacts first and fast. The left side logical brain is slower to respond. We do a lot of reacting, rather than responding, just by the default of human function. For example, as a mom, I struggle with being the listener who will keep my young adult daughter talking. She doesn't want to be judged, assisted, analyzed, coached, or counseled. She wants to be heard and understood. Period. But because I am so emotionally attached to her happiness and well-being, I forget to actively listen and make listening errors because I feel so protective and want to be her teacher. Oftentimes she reminds me, and then she becomes my teacher.

We can know all this relationship stuff, but when we get entangled emotionally with someone or something that really matters to us, our emotions can quickly take over our logic to respond appropriately. Just because we know better, we don't always DO better.

The book *Never Split the Difference: Negotiating as If Your Life Depended on It* begins with the simple premise that humans want to be accepted and understood. The most simple and effective concession we can perform to make that happen is active listening where we show empathy and sincere desire to better understand the other party and their experience. I stumbled upon this truth by chance at an appointment to close a deal for a business I was contracting with.

In my early twenties I was a software trainer for a company in Sudbury, Ontario. They were trying to win a big training contract with Bill, a client they had been unable to close. They sent me to close the deal. I wasn't on their sales team, nor did I know what to say once I got to Bill's office, so I just went on the sales call and listened.

I met with Bill in his beautiful corner office and spent an hour listening to him. I asked questions about the children in the photos hanging on the wall, the sailboat replica on his credenza, and about how and when he started his business. I was curious and I just asked a lot of questions and rephrased his answers back to him.

I recall at one point he spoke of issues in his business that our training would resolve, and I simply said, "We can help with that," but other than that, I just let him talk and talk and talk while I paid close attention to his message, nodded my head in agreement often, and restated a few things that I heard him say.

When I looked down at my watch and realized that an hour had gone by, I stood up to leave, walked to his office door, put my hand on the doorknob, and told Bill that our office would be in touch with him.

At that moment Bill said, "Oh Penny, I want you to know that you're the best conversationalist that I've had the pleasure to talk with in a very long time." I found it so interesting that I said nothing, he said everything, and yet he felt that **I** was the best conversationalist. I became rich, in a lesson that I've used for decades to build relationships. The greatest need of the human spirit is the need to FEEL understood, and people love to talk about their favorite subject . . . themselves! By me simply listening to Bill, and restating the things he said to me, he felt understood and we got the big training deal. My lesson still rhymes in my mind as this: Listening—*cha-ching!* (insert cash register sound here ☺).

Learning Conversations

When people come together to have difficult conversations, they tend to be thinking more about what they're going to say, versus what they're going to learn. Active listening gets you in the mindset that you are seeking to understand the situation from the other person's perspective, which will expand your understanding of what you know to be true already. When you hear their input, you advance to a new level of knowledge or information—therefore, if you have the chance to be the first listener, take it! Say nothing, hear everything, including what is not being said (body language, feelings, behavior), and then tell the person what you've understood so far.

Here's how I do it. While they're talking, I am focused on them, making eye contact, nodding or gesturing that I am following their every word. When they're finished talking, I say, "If I understood you correctly, you think that . . . or you feel that . . . [add a summary of what you heard]." They feel relief when they feel understood. Be the listener who filters out the facts and the feelings and other clues. You may even want to ask questions to elicit more details, but be careful not to hijack the conversation and make it about you. You can hope to get a chance to speak when it's your turn and have the same respect of listening modeled back to you.

Sift through the Message; Then Restate

Contrary to what most people think, the best communication skill is not coming out big with words but rather how you let others' words come in. When you seek to understand people, and tell them what you've heard them say, you'll be making friends, influencing people, and creating solid relationships, leaving people wanting more of YOU. This is another inside job, meaning you have responsibility and control over it, and it feels opposite of what seems natural when we're trying to be effective communicators and leaders.

Model of Communication

- Step 1: A sender sends a message.
- Step 2: A receiver receives it.
  [Reflection point—Has communication taken place at this point? Not yet, because there's no confirmation of understanding what was sent (said) versus what was heard (received). You need all four steps.]
- Step 3: The receiver restates what they heard, back to the sender.
- Step 4: The original sender confirms accuracy or tries again.

Listening could potentially save millions of dollars in the workplace because with clear communication, errors are reduced. Errors are costly. Instructions could be communicated until clearly understood the first time, eliminating unnecessary errors.

Relationships are strengthened when people are willing to hear each other out to the point of feeling better about strained situations or having healthy debates.

Barriers to Listening

There are quite a few things that get in the way of active listening. Internal and external distractions, judgment, analyzing, and advising are among the popular ones.

Distractions

Are you really present when you are listening? Distractions come in many forms. Multitasking, mind wandering, background noise, and interruptions can pull at our ability to hear and understand what is being communicated. We can manage many of these distractions by setting up our conversations in a quiet or private area, offering our full attention, and being mindful of our focus. Active listening requires your attention. If you don't have time to listen, put the conversation off to a better time in the very near future. If you missed what someone said because your mind wandered, ask them to repeat. "Can you repeat that last part? I don't think I caught what you said." People are willing to repeat when they know you're seeking to understand them.

Internal distractions can be barriers to listening as well. When your mind is running wild with your own stress, ideas, judgments, or analysis of what you are hearing, you're limiting your potential to restate, acknowledge, or validate what you've heard.

When people are communicating with each other, it's possible they're speaking and listening from the past programming of an old story. You know, one of those old limiting beliefs that we're unconsciously carrying around in our suitcase. You could be hearing someone's words and "already listening," hearing a different meaning than what's being communicated to you. For example, when someone gives you feedback, and you have an old story that says you're not enough, you may have to check in with yourself to ensure that you're hearing the facts and not the fiction from your old story.

Similarly, you can expect that whatever you say, others are hearing something different.[1] In negotiation with others, people get preoccupied thinking about what they are going to say, how they will respond to that last point they heard, or how they will frame their next argument. Misunderstandings and misinterpretations become very common, especially under the stress of a challenging conversation.

Judgment, Analyzing, and Advising

When we're judging, analyzing, or advising we're not actively listening. Those opportunities might come up later in the conversation; however, they are barriers or obstacles to the listening role in communication.

Judgment and opinions get in the way of listening. Why can't people just think and behave the way we do? Well, if they did, the world would be very boring and predictable. Humans are complicated, and we will never fully understand them. Could you adopt the idea that things you're hearing aren't right or wrong? They're not black or white? Or good or bad? They just are what they are. Someone's communication. Someone's feelings. Someone's perspective. From this point of neutrality, we can suspend judgment and analysis, comment on what we've heard, and feed the other person's greatest need, which is the feeling of being understood, regardless of whether we agree or disagree.

Other barriers to listening come in the form of giving advice: "You shouldn't worry about these minor things" or analyzing: "Maybe the other person is just having a bad day." Be mindful of your tendencies when you are listening, and try to just be wide open to let others' words come in. Create an energetic space for their conversation, meaning, clear your mind and just let them fill it.

The Talking Part of Active Listening

When you acknowledge what someone has said, you are demonstrating that you have heard them. You are mirroring back or paraphrasing what you heard and hopefully doing so in a manner that shows you care. The agenda of the conversation doesn't turn to you. Your feedback is just to clarify your listening. Acknowledgment statements could sound like this:

"What I heard you say is . . ."
"What I understand so far is . . ."
"Let me make sure I'm understanding what you are saying. . . ."
"Let me restate what I heard you say to make sure that I got it. . . ."

To validate means to recognize or affirm the validity or worth of a person's feelings. Validation is an act of helping someone feel understood. The difference between acknowledging and validating is in the emphasis on their feelings. Without judgment (right or wrong) or agreement, validation just allows the person to release and gain some form of normalcy in their situation. Validation statements might sound like this:

"I understand that you feel it wasn't appropriate for me to ask that question."
"You're furious because he went above you to your manager rather than coming to you directly."

In his book *I Hear You*, Michael Sorensen offers the benefits of validation to build extraordinary relationships. Effective validation can reduce frustration and fear, as well as enhance excitement in others.[2] It can also help you get others to listen to you, resolve disagreements, and deepen relationships. To be actively listening, you must do something more than just hear. You must **say** something.

The difference between acknowledging and validating is in the outcome where the one talking will feel more than just heard. They will feel valued and will continue to contribute to a solution. Imagine a brainstorming session where you are just hearing the contributions, and repeating them out loud, versus commenting.

"Fewer meetings." You acknowledge what you heard.

"Thank you for sharing that, Jason. Some feel that meetings are too frequent." You validate his response, not judging or agreeing, but building trust, confidence, and connection to keep the conversation momentum moving forward.

To be a great listener, you must also be a great validator. There are two main goals to validation:

1. To acknowledge a specific emotion
2. To offer justification for feeling that emotion

The opposite is to invalidate someone's feelings with our response, which is counterproductive, and can escalate difficult situations. Invalidating versus validating could sound like this:

Rather than invalidating with . . .
"It's not so bad; could have been worse; you're overreacting,"

validate with . . .
"That must be really difficult; I'm sorry you're going through this; sounds so frustrating."

Avoid becoming defensive and offering unsolicited advice, and accept responsibility for the emotion if appropriate.[3]

Communication to support healthy relationships is not always straightforward. Learning to recognize and practice validating versus invalidating statements can help you develop good rapport as well as understanding and productive conversations.

Understand Conflict to Dissolve It

Negotiations and conflict resolutions are more successful on a foundation of each party feeling understood. Some say to not give the other party much attention; however, a good negotiator does just the opposite.[4] If the other party doesn't understand, they may not believe that you've heard them, and will be less likely to hear your point of view, because they suppose that you have not grasped what they're trying to tell you.

Consider this first part of the negotiation, mediation, or conversation like leveling out the foundation of sand before you flip your castle mold upside down onto it. You want a solid foundation, right? No warps, no rocks, sticks, or toys in the way, just a smooth layer of level sand on which to build. That foundation is symbolic to each party seeking to understand the other first, which creates a solid new understanding from both parties to build agreements. Listen, acknowledge, and agree on what you can. There have been numerous mediations with clients of mine who spent 90 percent of our time together speaking and listening to each other, then as if some magic wave washed over them, all conflict dissolved, without any further negotiations or agreements made. In these cases, conflict resolve turned to conflict dissolved, just by understanding each other's points of view. Sometimes we can just agree not to agree on something and be content with seeing things from each other's viewpoint.

You'll be a seasoned negotiator if you seek to understand the other party first, and stay with it regardless of if they reciprocate. By focusing attention on the other party to ensure a feeling that they've been understood, you're helping them make their case. There are several techniques of paying close attention beyond restating or paraphrasing what's been said, including asking the other party to clarify what they mean, and requesting ideas be repeated if there is uncertainty.

You can reframe their communication positively, and from their perspective, adding strength and validity to their points. By doing this you're already making agreements. You agree that you heard what they said, and you may even agree with some things they say. You are in fact disarming them by allowing them space to vent their opinions and emotions, and that's fertile ground for further development.

Understanding Doesn't Mean Agreeing

It's possible to completely understand someone, and completely disagree with them.

Just remember that in the early stage of the conversation where intention is to seek to understand them fully, you're listening and making agreements on what you've heard them say, and anything else that you can agree on. You'll have time later in the conversation to state your reasons for disagreement with certain things. If you inject your disagreement too soon, you'll be interrupting the fundamental foundation of listening to understand.

Contrary to what you might feel compelled to do, to break through the other side's resistance, you must reverse the dynamic. If you want them to listen to you, you first listen to them. If you want their acknowledgment on your points, you can first acknowledge theirs, and if you want them to agree with you, then you will want to lead that behavior by finding ways to agree with them.[5]

The Third Story

They say that there are three sides to every story. My side, their side, and the right side. Well, there is some merit to that. I call it the third story.

To listen while in conflict, you almost have to take yourself out of character so you can filter the emotions from the facts. Try finding the third story by thinking about how things would look from the perspective of the teacher at the youngsters' sandbox. She's impartial and neutral and is helping kids sort out issues based on facts.

Imagine a time way back when you and a friend were kids, having a great time digging and building, and there is a teacher acting as a referee, standing over the sandbox, observing play. The referee has no emotional stake in the sandcastle or little dirt road system, or those who are building; they're just observing. This person would be synonymous to a third story . . . someone who has no investment in either side of the story that is playing out. They understand each side's concerns and act as a neutral observer, otherwise known as a mediator. They can remove judgment and describe the problem as a difference, rather than a who's right and who's wrong perspective. The difference is factual, and therefore both parties can buy into the description of the difference, which creates an opening to build upon.

Let's untangle the previous scenario from chapter 1 about Laura, the sales department manager who threw her colleague Tom under the bus, by understanding the three sides to their story. Here's what was originally said:

> Meeting chair: "Laura, did your sales department work harder to reach our projected target for widgets this quarter?"
> Laura: "I would like to report a sales increase; however, the quality of the widgets was substandard for market, and I asked Tom to deal with it at his department, but I never heard back."
> Tom: "You can't pin your poor sales and unproductive team on me."

Result: The whole room feels awkward. . . . Conflict brews between Laura and Tom.

From Laura's story—Laura, as the manager of the sales department, feels under pressure for sales and has been expected to increase numbers based on some projected targets, but her sales department is getting feedback from customers that the quality of the widgets is not as promised; therefore, the customers are not interested in ordering more. She is blaming quality control issues—specifically Tom—for not getting the quality up to standard for the sales numbers being low.

(Note: There is likely potential for more than three stories . . . because Laura may be packing around old stories in her suitcase, which causes her to speak and listen from old patterning. Can you see why problems get so entangled? And why it's important to clean up old stuff?)

From Tom's story—Tom, as manager of production, is dealing with obtaining supplies within his budget, and a team of staff who are mostly all new due to recent turnover. He's doing his best to output decent quality with the resources he has to work with. He feels that Laura is using him as a scapegoat, blaming him for her department's lack of productivity.

Laura spoke from her story. Tom spoke from his. This is a natural tendency; however, it breeds defensiveness because each one is speaking from their own story and blaming the other. There is conflict and resentment on both sides toward each other; they're disconnected, not working together, not collaborating, and their department personnel are feeling the undercurrent of the conflict.

Let's help them approach a conversation about it. Laura and Tom would be wise to find the third story in the situation, and lead from there. To find the third story, think about how things would look from the perspective of the referee in the sandbox. The description of the situation might be that the sales department is getting flak from customers about substandard product, and therefore reluctant to push sales of the widget. Production is challenged with limited resources, and Tom feels that the widgets produced for sale are of decent standard and not the cause of poor sales performance. (Notice how there is no judgment in this third story? No right or wrong, good or bad, just a pointing out of the difference between the opinions/perceptions of Laura and Tom.)

Getting to the third story takes active listening. One needs to clearly understand the other, and vice versa, for each other to feel understood, acknowledged, and legitimate in the conversation, but we typically begin conversations from our "story," describing our situation from our perspective. This usually triggers the very reactions that we're trying to avoid because it lands as a judgment toward the other person, which provokes defensiveness, and thus the downward spiral of a heated conversation spins.

Because this conflict is brewing, Laura and Tom must manage their relationship. They can choose to stay disconnected, but that's going to rear its ugly head over and over again, or they can choose to deal with it head-on, hopefully immediately.

Rather than Laura's opening line from inside her story ("I would like to report a sales increase, but the quality of the widgets was substandard for market, and I asked Tom to deal with his department, but I never heard back."), she would be opening a conversation based on acknowledging the description of the problem and inviting Tom to the conversation: *"Tom, I want to apologize for what happened in the manager's meeting earlier today. Can we talk? I want to explain what I feel is preventing sales of the widget and hear your perspective on the situation."*

By speaking from the third story, which is neutral, Laura likely would get buy-in from Tom to continue the conversation to clean up the mess. Go Laura!

Or Tom could initiate because he wants to take responsibility to create the workplace culture that he's part of. His third story approach could be, *"Laura, can we talk about what happened in the meeting? I was upset by what you said, and I want to explain what's bothering me and get your perspective as well."*

When we step into the third story to explore the other person's side, we don't have to step out of our own. It's just a more expanded, all-encompassing viewpoint to improve our understanding and perspectives. This is fertile grounds for HOLY SHIFTS because with this new perspective, we can immediately grow with what we've learned, into a new space for more productive conversation.

Listening from an objective (hard facts) posture rather than a subjective (personal perspective) posture will be beneficial to guide the dance through conflict to cooperation.

You don't need a mediator or referee to help you get to the third story. The key is in learning to find and describe the gap between each person's story, by removing the emotions and the judgment about who's right and who's wrong. It's a process of sifting out the facts from the emotions associated with the situation. The third person has an easier time to do this because they're not invested in the situation. Thinking like you are the one overseeing the situation can help you describe the difference between the two stories, which then become the agreeable point. What are Laura and Tom about to agree on?

- Feelings are hurt.
- There are competing priorities between sales and quality control.
- Customers are complaining and not reordering.
- The company needs sales.

From there, better conversations can get started. If conflict is still not resolved at this point, they're in a productive place to keep the conversation going for potential solutions.

Good to Great Listening

Ready for the big leagues of listening? Take your listening skills from good to great.

From their book *The New Extraordinary Leader: Turning Good Managers into Great Leaders*, authors Jack Zenger and Joseph Folkman distilled their best listening skills research to take us beyond the basics of not interrupting, following with facial expressions, and restating back what was said. Their *Harvard Business Review* article indicates that a skilled listener engages in a two-way active conversation to amplify, support, and provide constructive feedback.[6]

Asking a good question communicates back that one is listening and has comprehended it enough to want more information. This creation of a two-way dialogue promotes discovery and insight.

A safe environment where issues and differences can be discussed openly helps make the interaction a positive one. You want the speaker to feel supported and build their confidence, which doesn't happen if the listener is too passive or even slightly critical.

Great listeners can provide feedback without either party becoming defensive. If there are assumptions to challenge, the listener can contribute with the intention of trying to help, not win an argument.

Suggestions and input from the listener can be well received by the speaker if they feel supported. Where there is ongoing interaction in the conversation, the person speaking is more open to learn, rather than from someone silent through the whole conversation, then at the end has a suggestion, seems combative, or tries to give advice.

Although everyone can benefit from these tips to become a more skilled listener, they're especially important for managers, supervisors, and leadership of organizations.

The Remote Difference

Listening in the workplace has shifted because we aren't physically all in the same "place," and that trend is on the rise. Remote working statistics show an increasing percentage of remote workers and their desire to maintain work-from-home arrangements. During COVID-19, close to 70 percent of full-time workers were working from home. In the post-COVID-19 era, 92 percent of people surveyed expect to work from home at least one day per week and 80 percent plan to work at least three days from home per week.[7]

The typical problems to solve when managing relationships and productivity with remote workers are:

- Their lack of "feeling in on things"
- Their home-based challenges of either isolation or family 24/7
- Communication of issues (considering the absence of boardroom meetings and the informal avenues such as the watercooler or hallways)
- Lack of trust (both ways)
- Lack of connection, engagement, and retention

Solutions for strengthening relationships have not changed, but the medium for communication with remote employees has. Getting face-to-face on videoconference calls regularly for check-ins, both one-on-one as well as team meetings, can provide the connection that replaces in-person gatherings. Phone calls are a close second. Those working off-site need more connection time with their manager than the on-site folks to attain an equal feeling of being part of the team.

Focus on employee well-being first with regular check-ins, which are essential to build trust, ensure task prioritization, discuss roadblocks, and determine action items. The purpose of these check-in meetings is to listen. Ensure that individual needs are being heard and, where possible, addressed. The meeting rhythm for one-on-one conversations is recommended monthly in times of great change, or quarterly during more stable times. By helping people share concerns and feel connected despite their distance, they will adapt more effectively to change.

Check-ins can be short, sweet, and to the point. They will aid in accountability. This routine will help managers better understand the people under their wing. Create a meeting rhythm, put your listening ears on, and keep the connection strings tight.

We are living in a new era, and it's busier than ever with messages as well as demands on our attention, time, and energy. Listen to me, hear this, buy this, do this, own this, see this, don't do this, stay in, limit your exposure, wear a mask . . . but the greatest need of our human spirit is the need to feel understood. What if we just tried to really hear people, to receive THEIR message . . . to understand them, and to leave the conversation with them feeling better than they did before it started?

Practice sifting through others' words and hone the greatest communication skill of all, which is active listening. By offering validation rather than advice, analyzing, or minimalizing one's feelings, you'll help people find solutions to their problems and let go of their difficult emotions. You also may increase the chance that they will listen to you, but it's not a guarantee.

We won't resolve all conflicts or disagreements by listening. Sometimes the other person just isn't talking, they've picked up their toys and they're going home! We may not have control or influence, but we can have a very strong grounding to use our skills to the best of our ability.

Even if there aren't resolutions made, and more complex situations need third-party intervention to resolve issues, respectful communication and understanding each other's feelings and viewpoints are valuable because people will know that they care about each other and, if nothing else, can separate disagreements from the importance of the relationship. Separating the person from the problem is valuable. Just because we don't agree, doesn't mean we no longer like/love each other.

Did you discover any listening opportunities to HOLY SHIFT your workplace relationships? This is an opportunity for a HOLY SHIFT in your mindset and behavior. Write them down where you will see them often or download our worksheet companion, put them into action, and let the sifting begin!

4

Yield to Your WHY

Ground yourself in purpose.

WHAT IS YOUR WHY?

Do you remember how inquisitive you were as a kid? Were you always asking why? "Why is the sky blue, Mommy? Why does he have more toys, Daddy? Why is the water leaving the hole we made in the sand? Why this? Why that?" Why everything? Kids are curious, and we forget how powerful that curiosity is until we understand the power of WHY.

We all have significant WHY power. WHY power is the internal force that comes from within. It's our passion, our purpose, our reason for being who we want to be and doing what we do. We forget it exists, but it's always there, sometimes buried deep under many layers of status quo, other people's expectations, or day-to-day mundane routines.

Stronger Than Your Willpower

Your *WHY power* is stronger than your *willpower*. Sometimes all we have during difficult situations is a reason that is stronger than we are. Perhaps it's a social cause, a professional standard, an important relationship, or a precious family. There are many WHYs, and each of us has a unique set of these important driving factors that help us stay grounded and strong during the harshest sandstorms, especially when our emotions are spinning out of control.

You'll know you need to tap into your WHY power when you feel stuck. Perhaps it's the resistance to change, or dealing with things that you've been putting off, or setting boundaries for yourself, or saying no, or letting go. Perhaps it's the discomfort of unpacking what you see in your suitcase or deciding to have that challenging conversation to resolve some conflict. All these examples have one thing in common . . . they're uncomfortable, and to reach a resolve, you'll need self-motivation to move out of your comfort zone, through the internal or external conflict, and into something better.

The ironic thing about our "comfort zone" is that it really isn't that comfortable at all. It's just familiar. The fact that you're thinking about making a change is proof that you're choosing something of better comfort, but if you want a different result, you'll have to **do** something different, and that usually entails getting clear on WHY it matters.

Are you clear on your WHY?

What are you passionate about?
Why do you work at the career you've chosen?
Why does your work matter?
What do you believe?
What do you want?
What do you stand for?

Exploring these questions helps uncover the gold that not only inspires you but inspires other people also.

Finding our deepest WHY usually strikes an emotional chord. I call it the WHY that makes you CRY. If you can get to that depth of passion, then you're there. You've uncovered and discovered a mighty force within yourself. Tap that. Often!

Let me share a personal conflict and the WHY that helped me overcome it.

Strength through a Sandstorm

Back in 2014, I had to manage my emotions and behavior through a sweet relationship that went sour. It all started when I chose to end a sixteen-year-long relationship with the father of my children. I was out of integrity with the message I teach and the life I lived. My partner and I couldn't seem to connect, communicate, or stay committed to the processes suggested by therapists, so I walked away. Me, the relationship guru, threw in my towel, and it caused upset with our children. One of them took sides with their father and chose not to speak to me for many painful years. I had to learn to stand in the decisions I made despite the rumor mill in our small town, the alienation from that former partner and our circle of friends, all while bending, flexing, and feeling totally out of control. I was angry and heartbroken.

A good friend of mine, Barry Spilchuk, noticed that I was holding on to the situation very tight. He suggested that I *"let it go, so that God could pick it up."* I never forgot that. That became my HOLY SHIFT: having faith that if I held the intention of what I wanted, and more importantly WHY it mattered, and let go of the need to control the timing, it would work out just as it was supposed to. And so I did. I let go of the tight grip I had on needing connection with my child, I let go of the rumors people were spreading about me, and I let go of the need to control details or force my child to reconnect with me. I let it all go. The pain did not go, but my need to control the situation was let go. It was a decision, not a feeling. It was brutally difficult, and it left an emptiness that I would never wish upon any human being.

My WHY was the example I wanted to set for my children. It was for them that I wanted to demonstrate what a loving relationship looked like. I knew from my parents, I knew it was possible, I knew it took two, and I was ending dysfunction in hopes for a better tomorrow.

Despite the disconnect with my child, I loved anyway. I stood in who I wanted to be regardless of who was joining me or supporting me. I shared my most painful emotions with my closest circle of people, and I cried and yearned for things to be better. In those times, I learned about the fragility of relationships, of how quickly something so sweet could go sour. I grew, painfully, but I expanded, became stronger and more resilient.

Have you ever felt disconnected from someone important to you?

Ever wait for your phone to ring?

For your text to ding?

For a sign that someone you are really missing connection with is reaching out to you?

For an invitation to resolve a disconnect, or for your invitation to reconnect to be acknowledged?

Did you ever wait to be invited in to play in a sandbox you've been feeling excluded from?

I began to position myself for the best play I knew, and went straight inward to the foundation of my WHY for strength. As I started unpacking my suitcase of fears, insecurities, and painful emotions, I uncovered the root of this conflict and I figured out the tools and strategies to resolve it, within myself. As I applied my new insights and strategies to my life, something miraculous started to happen. My child slowly started reaching out to me.

It took a while to get there, but almost three years later, two days before Christmas, the doorbell rang. My handsome eighteen-year-old son was standing at the door. I'll never forget the feeling of being whole as he walked through the door to join my daughter and me for the first time in what felt like a lifetime. Until that moment, I never understood the power of WHY. But when I saw my son staring back at me on that snowy day at Christmastime, I knew I had discovered something truly transformational.

Resolution is a work in progress; it doesn't always happen overnight. I often say that love is easy, but relationships are hard. My kids are my WHY. They are the reason of importance to do what's right, even if there are consequences, and even if it doesn't feel good.

I've learned that even the relationship experts don't win them all, but there's no such thing as a failed relationship if you learn the lessons. My lessons were clear. I needed to maintain a position of integrity and take responsibility for making the family relationships work as best I could, without throwing sand. I needed to know what issues were mine. I have a suitcase—remember my old stories of not being good enough? And I also needed to remind myself that I'm a great mom, regardless of the situation. I needed to have faith that my WHY power was enough.

Even though this conflict happened in my personal life, it made me realize that it was the best possible lesson I could have ever received as a conflict and relationship expert. Before this, I thought I knew all there was to know about handling conflict, but through this experience, I learned that all the strategies in the world won't help without a strong grounding in the reason that resolution matters.

What happened next was I started sharing the story of how I resolved this painful personal conflict during some of my leadership training sessions, and I was shocked by the response I got. Leaders came up to me after sessions, admitting that they too were not only struggling with work conflicts but struggling in their personal relationships as well.

When I started applying the insights, tools, and strategies that got me through this difficult conflict with my son with my coaching and training programs, suddenly I was coaching high-level leaders at a whole other level.

I realized that all people, regardless of where they sit on an organizational chart, needed this higher-level understanding about resolving conflict from the inside out.

The clarity of your WHY will help you stay grounded through the most severe sandstorms, or the most difficult inner work, like unpacking your suitcase. WHY is the magic quest. It's at the center, or the core of everything. Ask it over and over again to get deeper and deeper meaning to your own passion and purpose. There are reasons beyond the reasons that you think, feel, and behave a certain way. When you get really clear on the powerful WHY that makes you stay committed to the course of change, you can deal with any "what" that might come along and try to hijack your process.

The WHY at Your Core

In Simon Sinek's *Start with Why*, he draws a golden circle, based on the golden ratio,[1] a historical concept intersecting truth, beauty, and math.[2] This golden circle uses harmonious proportions to nest a small center circle labeled *Why*, inside a medium circle labeled *How*, inside a larger outer circle labeled *What*.

Sinek's inside-out concept suggests that we can achieve more when we start everything from the center circle of WHY, before even considering the how and the what. The concept can be used as a guide to improve leadership, corporate culture, product development, and sales and marketing.[3] His main point is that "people don't buy WHAT you do, they buy WHY you do it."[4]

Using the same concept to think inside the box of ourselves as individuals, getting clear on our WHY, our purpose, our cause, our reason for getting out of bed in the morning, is a very worthwhile place to start anything.

Sinek's golden circle is not just a communications hierarchy. The principles are grounded in the evolution of human behavior. It's not just an opinion, it's biology. Looking at a cross section of the brain, you'll see a similar set of nested circles where the outer circle, the neocortex, manages our rational and analytical thoughts and language (the WHAT). The inner circle is the limbic brain responsible for our feelings, like trust and loyalty, our behavior, and decision-making. The limbic brain has no capacity for language, which explains why people have trouble speaking about their WHY, their feelings, and their decisions. It's easier for our brain to give language to rationality and logic because they both sit in the same area of the brain.[5]

When we communicate from the inside out, from the clarity of WHY, we speak directly to the part of our brain that controls decision-making and the language that allows us to rationalize those decisions. For example, have you ever tried to explain why you love someone? Beyond their talent or their beauty, we love someone because of how they make us feel, but those feelings are difficult to articulate. The same is true for decisions. Sometimes we just have a gut feeling that a decision is right, but we have a hard time explaining why. It's not that we don't know why we decided a certain thing, it's that we have a trouble expressing the language.

Our limbic brains know the right thing, but due to our lack of ability to verbalize it, we create doubt. The power of this limbic brain is quite astounding to drive our behavior and help us control those actions or inactions born out of emotions like fear and hate. If you find yourself in a conflict or relationship stalemate, tap into that inner limbic brain that won't mislead you, and ask the deeper question of WHY?

Why does this relationship matter?

Why should I move through the fear or hatred?

Asking WHY a Conflict Is Worth Resolving

A good use of the question WHY is to determine if a conflict is worth the effort to resolve, or if bringing up the conversation is worth the potential argument that may ensue.

Is this issue worth the energy? If it's keeping you up at night, renting space in your head, or percolating inside you like an old pot of coffee, then yes! Decide whether you're going to address the issue or not. Is it a big deal? Can you let it go? Should you let it go? You may want to think about it from the professional standards or ethical framework of your profession. Is this against the integrity of who you are and what you stand for?

Get to your WHY. Why does it matter to you? What value is causing you discomfort and ultimately, driving you into action? Because your WHY power is stronger than your willpower, leveraging it can create motivation or a sense of obligation to speak up.

Why Should I Stand Up for Myself?

We can find strength to say no, let go, and set healthy boundaries for ourselves when we are clear on our WHY. Use it as solid ground to stand up to people who want to dominate or intimidate you.

I asked a trusted friend and resilient leader what he remembered about the early sandbox. "There was always a bully," he said without hesitation. Ah yes, the one who wants to rule the roost, serve up mud patties, throw sand, and try to push people over like a bulldozer. Today's workplaces are not immune to bullies who use words or actions to show dominance. They can offend, embarrass, humiliate, or demean a worker or group of workers. Their behavior intimidates, isolates, or discriminates against their target. Workplace bullying, lateral violence, harassment including sexual harassment are definite definitions of what PLAY NICE does NOT mean. Being a victim or witness and doing nothing about it also does not mean playing nice. Dealing with issues to get to the root of them, correcting or resolving them **IS playing nice**. We need to stand up, speak up, and document behavior that goes against employment law, which in Canada is the Canadian Centre for Occupational Health and Safety;[6] in the United States of America, the Department of Labor follows the Civil Rights Center.[7]

Defined as "engaging in a course of vexatious comment or conduct against a worker [that is known] to be unwelcome,"[8] workplace harassment also includes psychological or personal harassment.[9] The conduct could happen even just once, but typically happens over a period of time. Lateral violence[10] in the workplace is defined as anger or rage toward one's peers rather than one's adversaries.

It's interesting to note that we all have bully-type characteristics, when we have an intention to impose our will on another person. They're often used through positions of authority; take, for example, a parent who says to their child, "Eat your dinner or you're going to bed."

Regardless of how other people's behavior affects us, we don't have to be subjective to it, but we should speak to it.[11] When? About as fast as rumble strips along the center lanes of our highways keep us from crossing over the line. The trauma that people endure from these types of harassments can cause long-term effects; so, like the rumble strips, if the behavior goes out of bounds, let the rumbling sound! Gloria did not. Here's the long-term effect.

Gloria put up with four years of being bullied at her career in the military. She was fighting so hard that she didn't even realize she was getting sick, until the day she became really sick. She said that she could have easily stayed in the grips of depression, but the day she started crying as she just looked at her uniform was her day of giving in, realizing that the bullying had won.

She left the military for a teaching job that she loved so much she'd have done it for free, and although she wasn't being bullied anymore, she was exposed to bully-like behaviors, which were triggering old thoughts about the trauma she'd lived through. She left that job for that reason. She just didn't have the resolve that she used to, to deal within the environment long-term. Although she could hold her ground and stand up to and speak up to situations, she just lacked the resilience and desire to stay in a workplace that had the right conditions to set off her triggers. Today she feels as though she's living in remission, that although there's no evidence of disease, she doesn't feel she's cured.

Even though the workplace relationships and challenging conversations were 80 percent successful, she preferred an offer to work from home where she could be completely in control of her surroundings. Because she was so far down in the depths of bullying throughout her past, things that would seldom trigger her spun her around like a Tasmanian devil and she just never wanted to go back to "those times." As sad as it made her to recount her journey and how it affected her future life even distant from the old career and people, she also shared gratitude for her very empathetic understanding of others who have gone through a similar storm, where previously she would have encouraged people to *suck it up*. Having gone through it herself, she knows what it's like to carry forward.

Here's an opposite story. Trent DID stand up to bulling in high school and brought these same lessons into his career. As a twelve-year-old eighth-grade student, Trent found himself awkwardly trying to fit into a school with twelve- to twenty-year-olds, nestled within a Portuguese community of Bristol, Rhode Island. Trent was three things that most students were not: tall, blond, and polite. To mend a hairline fracture to his clavicle, Trent had to wear a thick brace over his shoulders, with clasps on both the front and back; he was teased about "wearing a bra," tormented by several male students, and name-called things like "gay," those bullying words that used to—and still do—plague our schools today.

Right in algebra class, Trent mouthed something back to a hot-headed student, Manny, who made a rude comment. Manny came at him with his fists ready, Trent stood up to him and punched him right in the face. Manny was out cold, the school nurse got called, the principal's office was involved, and Trent found himself on a two-week detention. Even in the detention, he was being accosted by male student friends of Manny, and day after day Trent had to wrestle his way out of strongholds, throw a few punches, and run fast to escape the small gangs that waited for him to exit the schoolyard and get home. Still, he always managed to hold his ground, and quite a few of the gang boys suffered bruises, especially to their ego. Manny's gang of boys enlisted an older boy—*Fish* was his name—to beat up Trent. He was bigger than the rest and had a reputation of being a heavy hitter. News of Fish's involvement spread through the entire school. A swarm of students stood in a big circle, Trent was caught trying to flee the schoolyard and found himself facing Fish for a fight. There were a few punches thrown back and forth when Trent got thinking of a strategy. "I'm not going to win this fight. There are too many guys, and a circle of students between me and my home." With the next punch, Trent purposely went down onto the ground and said, "You win. You beat me. You won." The boys circled Fish like he had just won a victory prize. Trent was never bothered by them again, and recalls, "It was giving into the fight that won me back my dignity. I didn't have to hide in the hallways or constantly figure out how I was going to exit the safety of school and get home.

"I have a sharp enough mind, pretty quick wit, and I've used that lesson to realize that I might not win every fight of negotiation going straight forward, because like two rams hitting each other head on, no one really wins. I've learned that sometimes you have to lose a little bit to give the other person the victory that they need so that you can move forward. Fish and his group got the little modicum of victory that they needed. They were a tough group of kids who were having their egos taunted and teased for not being able to beat this tall, blond, polite kid up, and so by giving them a piece of what they needed, there was resolution, and it was acceptable for me," Trent said.

Trent is now an owner and CFO of a large firm and a speaker on the topic of resilient leadership. He uses the opportunity to move negotiations forward by finding win-win situations, by seeing opportunities to advance business relationships by standing up to those who use bully tactics, and also by giving people some of what they need, so the solution toward win-win can move forward.

The violence in the story that played out four decades ago is not acceptable by today's standards, but it still goes on. In the workplace, bullying comes in different forms, but the underlying bully beliefs are about dominance, about staking their position whether it be for negotiating or not, and is usually done out of insecurity. The more someone's insecurity is rocked, the more threatened they feel, which is counterproductive, so you'll want to find ways that go in the opposite direction to offer something more favorable for them. Taking a stand requires setting your own boundaries about how you'll allow others to treat you.

Setting Healthy Boundaries

Do you know why a sandbox has walls? They're boundaries to keep the sand contained within, so that everyone can have a safe and healthy environment to play in. We all carry a responsibility and have a role to play in keeping workplaces safe and healthy. Workers who see a health and safety problem have a duty to report the situation to their employer or supervisor, who in turn is required to address the problem. Like the sandbox walls, boundaries are healthy.

I'll bet that if you ever played with sand and water, you made a castle and moat (a ditch that surrounded it filled with water, intended as a defense against attack). If you'd like to be more powerful, efficient, and effective and protect your integrity, then you'll need to set boundaries, just like a moat, which will help you feel safe and therefore able to define and communicate your expectations to others.

Max, a client whom I coach, asked me how to deal with a colleague who did not respect a process of safely maintaining equipment. I suggested that Max set firm boundaries with his colleague about the process in place to maintain the equipment. I also advised Max to schedule a brief meeting to reinforce the process and explain why it was critical to the roles, goals, and mission of the team, and to ask his colleague for any input or feedback that could enhance the process.

"Once your process is established, don't bend with the results," I said. "People need to feel your expectations and boundaries by your consequences. If you're wishy-washy with your own boundaries, others will be as well. Be firm and fair."

Max returned to his workplace, set his boundaries in his own mind, respectfully communicated them to his colleagues, and asked for input and compliance. The employees did what was expected of them, and the organization's boundary held up long into the future.

Problems arise when leaders are loose. Don't forget: We're all leaders. A team's performance can get sloppy when its members stop taking full responsibility for their tasks, and when there are no consequences. Boundaries are like consequences. A team lead could tighten the boundaries, visit the issues, model the appropriate behavior, and ask that it be followed. But don't wait for the team lead to tackle all these leadership roles. Dig in! Ask the team lead if and how you can help, or give them your great ideas on what you'd recommend. When you directly address the poor procedure instead of blaming or avoiding the conversation, you're sending a message that you're committed to fair, safe, and profitable play.

Just like children inside the confines of a sandbox feel safe, or the townsfolk of a medieval city feel protected inside the fortress from outsiders, adults need to feel boundaries to find their safe zones too, and they'll push until they meet the resistance before they feel secure. Boundaries are protection for all.

When my yellow lab Joy was a puppy, we attended obedience school, where James, a strict trainer, helped me realize that I was giving Joy too much freedom to do what *she* wanted to do, and that I had to exercise firm boundaries so that she could experience immediate consequences to behavior that needed correction, and immediate praise for obedient behavior. James took the leash and demonstrated by correcting her jumping up on people. I stood in front of Joy, and when she tried to jump up on me, James corrected her with a rattle of her choker chain. He asked me to repeat; I did, Joy did, and James did the same thing. On the third attempt she obeyed and was praised by James. I was surprised how quickly the training took effect. Furthermore, Joy looked up to the trainer for praise and befriended him. "See, Penny?" said James. "She still likes me. Dogs want a strong leader, and she respects me for being firm."

People are not as forgiving as dogs, nor do we want to treat them as such at work; however, they do need boundaries and they respect those who set and maintain firm and fair ones to correct bad behavior. They also perform well and respect leaders who give immediate and specific praise for a job well done.

Manager tip: Help your team understand "why" an issue is important or valuable. People (especially millennial and centennial generations) are curious to know the bigger picture of how their roles and behaviors matter in the grand scheme of things.

It's not easy to set and maintain boundaries in your life. There have been people whom I've discontinued business with because I didn't feel they respected my boundaries. I've discontinued friendships and relationships where my boundaries were being violated. The better news is that I have found better business and personal relationships that honor and respect who I am and what I'm intending to accomplish. **We teach people how to treat us.** It's up to us to set our boundaries and build that moat—not walls to keep us from getting out, or prevent others from getting in, but a safe space for us to build our greatest castle.

Often your greatest answers are found in the clarity of your WHY. Tap into the strong grounding of purpose to guide you through the tough times. Saying no, letting go, setting boundaries, and teaching people how to treat you are challenging, and you need the inspiration and motivation of your WHY power.

When you're feeling stuck, tap the answers from the WHY center of your brain to help you move through fear. The question of why will also help you discern whether to act on resolving a conflict or let it go.

By the way, an update on the relationship between my son and me . . . we have a new relationship today. It's a work in progress; we gather regularly around food, usually bacon. It's amazing what you can attract when you cook a pound of bacon. The best feeling came when I was asked to come visit him at university; not only was I ecstatic to be invited, but I was even more excited to go get my suitcase, which just got a little lighter.

Spend a moment to write and clarify your WHY. Write it down where you will see it often or download our worksheet companion for HOLY SHIFTS that you discover while reading each chapter. Reminding yourself of your WHY power will help you stay grounded through the sandstorms.

5

Nurture Relationships

People who feel valued perform well.

ARE YOUR RELATIONSHIPS GROWING OR DYING?

Positive Polly was the one in your early sandbox who would make you gleam with pride when she complimented your sandcastle or toys, or when she tasted your mud pie with the "nom, nom, nom yummy!" response. It makes good sense to validate people and acknowledge the good, because by nurturing someone, we enhance our relationship with them.

The new workplace sandbox needs more nurturing than prepandemic times because the sudden shift created by the lockdown, closures, remote working, and digital collaboration has exposed and amplified the stretched-thin, worn-out, and burned-out status of our workforce.[1] It's a crucial time to help ourselves and others feel happier and healthier at work. Nurturing relationships can prevent unnecessary conflict, stress, and burnout, and, as they say, an ounce of prevention is worth a pound of cure.

Nurturing is a verb, an action of caring for or protecting someone while they are growing. Our human nature is to grow. Author Steve Siebold says, "You're either growing or dying. Stagnation does not exist in the universe."[2] Relationships are similar. They're either growing or they're dying. They don't stay status quo. This chapter will cover the nuances of mutual respect, verbal recognition, and constructive feedback in this new era of hybrid workers to keep the emotional buckets of work teams full. With some tweaks to prepandemic practices, nurturing is simple when relationships are going well, but how do you continue to nurture relationships when things are not going so well? Learning the steps to plan for good outcomes of challenging conversations will have everlasting value, because relationships are important and clearing the obstacles along the way is a necessary part of interdependence.

Respect

Respect means admiring someone's qualities, abilities, or achievements, and having a true regard for their feelings, rights, wishes, or traditions. The Latin origin of the word *respect* breaks it down to *re*, which means "back" or "repeat," and *specere*, which means "to look at." To *respect* means to look at again, and in that relooking, to see someone we may be challenged by with fresh eyes, as a person who is worthy of a positive perspective or regard. Respect is another one of those inside jobs, another example of moving in the opposite direction of what we naturally feel like doing when we're conflicting with someone else.

Our natural tendencies are to match the energy that someone dishes out to us. If they disrespect us, we want to disrespect them. If they reject us, we feel like rejecting them. If they attack us, we feel like attacking back, because out of pain, we naturally want to cause pain back; however, this is a mutually destructive cycle with no end, which causes great loss for all involved. Just because someone doesn't deserve our respect doesn't mean we shouldn't give it.

During a workday, there are opportunities for behaviors to trigger a misalignment of relationships. To nurture relationships during these times, we can start with the basis of respect. This doesn't mean that we approve or like the other person's behaviors, but it does mean that we can choose to respond in a way that will honor other people's dignity and their basic humanity; we are able to make the choice to give respect first, even though we're not feeling it from them. Easier said than done!

To act respectfully or not is a behavior usually based on a feeling, but we don't always feel like it, especially when we're upset or angry with someone. It's easy to understand why in heated situations, we're not always feeling like being respectful, and we behave in ways that are contrary. We're human and reactive at first, and the first point of defense in conflict isn't always the rational option.

When you have antagonistic feelings, how do you turn them to respect? Start within.

Respect is better nurtured from within than forced. Although showing respect to another person is a behavior, its foundation within us is an attitude. As Stephen Covey says, "you can't change the fruit without changing the root." Nurturing our own self-respect by taking responsibility for our own Positioning that we bring to the sandbox, Lightening our own load so we're not reacting from an old story, Actively listening to understand people, and Yielding to our WHY (all the strategies we've talked about so far) will help us get closer to developing the attitude of respect within, which will influence our behavior outward toward others.

Ask yourself why respecting the other person matters. Remember the strong WHY power energy that you can tap into when you feel stuck. There is likely a reason this person(s) is in your sandbox. They may be stakeholders like employees or colleagues you need to collaborate with, clients who are important to the success of the business, upper managers who hold authority of your career advancement, or even family members whom you never chose, but they're a part of the community you find yourself in. Given that they're in your sandbox, respecting them probably has some value for you. Dig there.

Here is some great incentive: When we respect others' humanness, we are respecting our own at the same time. When we respect the dignity of other human beings, we are respecting our own dignity in the process; therefore, the more respect we give out, the more we receive in the long run. Other nurturing skills like inclusion, empathy, and forgiveness are covered in later chapters.

Retain Remote Workers with Respect

In a survey done by Pew Research Center, the majority of workers who quit a job in 2021 cited feeling disrespected as one of the top reasons.[3] The challenge to retain people has been amplified by the remote and hybrid arrangements now common in our changing world of work. Respecting people's worth creates a feeling of respect that helps them perform better and feel better. According to an *MIT Sloan Management Review* article,[4] there are two distinct types of respect at work: The first is the baseline level that people feel entitled to as valued members of a team, and the second is the respect that can be earned for meeting or exceeding work expectations.

Although the meaning of *respect* has not changed, the shift to remote work has created the need for a different approach for respect to be more effective. Prior to the pandemic, signs of respect could be very subtle: social cues and gestures such as saying hello, holding a door, or casually sharing credit for successes. These gestures became contagious when others observed them and modeled the same; however, without an in-person environment, employees who work remotely focus more on tasks and less on interaction with others, so the subtle social cues aren't noticed.

There is a common feeling among remote workers of "out of sight, out of mind." Making an effort to communicate respect more often to those who are not physically in the workplace is going to increase their sense of being respected.

Managers can perform quick check-ins regularly in a method that the employee finds valuable. Some may prefer messages on a digital collaboration platform like Microsoft Teams or Slack, whereas others value a short phone call. The purpose of the check-in could be to ensure that remote employees have the resources they need to get their work done and to show a genuine interest in how they are doing as people. Managers can also be aware of the need to provide prompt responses for an employee who may be stuck waiting for an answer to be able to move forward with their project. Even if an answer is not available, a short and timely response to let them know you're working on it can save them hours of stress.

Remote workers want their time respected. Help them with flex time to accommodate family needs such as morning routines like getting children on or off the bus. The level of stress this could relieve for a working parent is huge. Minimize their interruptions by consolidating questions or messages and by using email rather than holding unnecessary meetings.

Never underestimate the power of validation or recognition to show appreciation for the work people do. When specific work and its related success can be acknowledged and connected to one's individual performance, there's a great deal of empowerment. Be specific, explicit, and intentional when validating remote employees' work with details of what they did and why it was done well. A thank-you goes a long way, as does a quick check-in where the only agenda is appreciation or to highlight their great work.

Offering regular feedback that validates progress being made by an employee who is making small steps toward a larger goal will help them feel confident and capable moving forward. The regularity will also help managers keep remote worker contributions top of mind. Just because an employee is remote doesn't mean they're contributing any less.

Sending tangible items such as physical greeting cards, sweets, birthday cakes, or gift cards goes a long way. Everyone likes to get a surprise in the mail that is not an advertisement or a bill to pay.

Everyone in the workplace can help to increase remote workers' visibility, and that's the goal when it comes to respect. Compliment their work publicly, include senior management on emails of accolades, invite them to meetings that are above their level in the company to make a presentation or provide a report, and give them a shout-out in meetings to remind those in person that there are people behind the scenes who are doing very valuable work.

When implementing these respect signals, be sure to find a cadence that is right for you and your team. A strategy that you can begin, do well at, and maintain going forward will sustain respect long into the future.

Recognition

With an attitude of respect, it's also easier to find the good in people and to recognize them for their value. Recognition is to know again, to remember or be reminded of the acknowledgment of a service. People are performing services all around us. Are we verbalizing our recognition for them enough? I've surveyed thousands upon thousands of audience members and the results are . . . drum roll please . . . NO we don't. And those people surveyed can't tell me why. We feel an expectation or entitlement for people or things to be a certain way and when they are, we say nothing, but when they're not, we're all over it. We need to turn that inside out.

People who feel good about themselves produce good results, so they feel even better about themselves, so they produce even better results, and the cycle of contagious enthusiasm goes onward and upward. We can influence productivity and potential by helping people feel good about themselves.

If that's not enough to motivate you to verbalize the value of other people, understand that there's also a dynamic exchange of good vibes when you give a compliment. You become rich in your own self-worth, having just helped someone else strengthen their sandcastle with each grain of confidence you help them see, feel, and understand about themselves.

The Compliment That Catapulted My Career

One compliment changed the trajectory of my whole career. It started at the ripe old age of eighteen when I was a secretary to Peter, the VP of a profitable sales company in Toronto. He always made me feel great by praising and acknowledging my work, which made me want to work harder and be better because the recognition was like food for my soul. It was quite a different message from the old "I'm not good enough story" in my suitcase.

One day, I learned the power of being the giver of recognition. I was out on my lunch hour shopping on Yonge Street in downtown Toronto, when I complimented the shoe store attendant for great service. It felt so good to be on the giving side of well-deserved praise that

I ran back to the office tell Peter. Another VP, Phil, was in his office when I told the story.

Within six months, Phil left the company we worked for and became the president of another. He called me personally to invite me to join his company because I was *"dynamite with people."* I was flattered, walked right into his compliment, and accepted the part-time opportunity to work in a direct sales business. Over the next decade I built and led my own sales team into their Million Dollar Club and learned about leading people who were self-employed, using recognition, education, and motivation. We need those three elements in our leadership today more than ever, three decades later, because people are still human, and their need for recognition, growth, and motivation hasn't changed. To compliment and be complimented is like feeling the sun from both sides.

Believe it or not, compliments and positive acknowledgments are useful in dispute resolution as well. Confirmed by my professors at the Harvard Negotiation Institute, even when you're sitting across the table entangled in conflict with someone, you can still verbally recognize the good in them. It might be a time where you're clouded with negative emotions, but remembering why you got into relationship with them in the first place will help you realize that there was something you liked about them in the beginning.

People are creatures of emotion, driven by pride and vanity. You just can't go wrong paying an honest compliment that someone has earned and deserves.

When you love people, you have no time to judge them. —Mother Teresa

Giving and Receiving Feedback

This is the most missed step in human relations. When we are open to really receiving what someone is putting out, when we have no resistance to their "gifts," we can keep the circle of energy flowing. Not all gifts are wrapped in fancy paper. Some gifts are hard to look at, painful to hold, or uncomfortable to unpack, but they are sometimes the most important gifts that we can receive because they expand and help us see things about ourselves that we need to see and grow through. Feedback is a gift.

When it comes to the dynamic energy between people, there is only one channel of energy, and we cannot be selective of that which we receive and that which we resist. We must take it all. It's how we unpack it and handle all that is within our control. Listening is an example. Receiving feedback is another one. It's not always easy to hear someone's opinion of us or our work or our ideas, but if we are open to receive it as a gift, we'll see it in a whole new light. The easiest way to receive feedback is to say thank you.

Nurturing relationships by receiving feedback can be an excellent engagement strategy. I interviewed Canada's recognition expert, Sarah McVanel of Greatness Magnified,[5] who helps companies retain their top talent through recognition. I asked her to share a story about a team that turned a corner, using recognition as a strategy.

According to an employee satisfaction survey, this department officially had the least satisfied and engaged team in the organization. The sterilization unit was plagued with dissatisfied employees, reports of bullying, and sick leave statistics that were off the charts, so they called in the expert to help them turn things around.

Being in a pivotal department in the organization, team members heard loud and clear when things went wrong, but rarely ever heard what went right. They lost hope that their ideas were worth sharing, they didn't feel valued, and some of them couldn't stand being in the same room as others. There were logistics issues as well. A windowless basement, isolated from the rest of the organization, and uniforms, hairnets, and gloves that stripped them of their individual identity.

In a team huddle, Sarah determined that people were afraid to communicate with each other for fear of being yelled at, and they hadn't been acknowledged in a while, so she began to facilitate their HOLY SHIFT by encouraging people to meet with her one-on-one, confidentially, to speak up about what they saw was working and what was not. This was a recognition of both the strengths and the weaknesses. Once the team members felt they were heard, they felt supported enough to move forward, as if a seed of hope was planted in the sand, instead of the turd of some cat . . . which was the old normal.

When the employees felt that they were being understood by their leaders, and that their concerns mattered, they became more open to finding solutions. It took conversations and focus to draw a line in the sand, and shift into something new, but with some strategy and effort coaching, the team moved the engagement needle from the worst to the most satisfied team in the organization.

Fast-forward to today, we are in a current talent shortage, so the most direct way to retain and engage people is by giving them what they want. People want to be **respected**, they want to be **recognized**, and they want to be heard and accepted as a valuable part of the whole.

Team engagement is everyone's responsibility. Organizations sometimes have corporate swag like T-shirts, hats, plaques, or even gold watches to recognize years of service, but the richest opportunities to nurture each other sit with every one of us, every single day to *respect* and *recognize* and *receive* each other . . . all of which mean, in their original word forms, to revisit or relook at the situation in some way to understand it with patience and humility.

We don't have to wait for a top-down approach to recognize people, nor do we have to wait a year or even twenty-five years to celebrate loyalty. We just have to keep these concepts top of mind, and practice them regularly.

Balancing the Relationship Account

Relationships are like bank accounts. They require regular deposits to stay positive and to keep appreciating, because every now and then we need to make a withdrawal on the relationship bank account we have with others.

Withdrawals come in many forms. Perhaps we need to ask someone for a favor or for support, to give back to us, or we need to have a difficult conversation to correct behavior or resolve some conflict. To make sure that the relationship doesn't go bankrupt, we need to have a healthy positive balance in the account.

Deposit options are endless, and so is the effect. Respect, words of praise, kind acts that serve others, a smile, even a prayer or thoughts of good intention go a long way. Most deposits that have lasting impact on interpersonal relationships have no financial cost. They're just an expression of thought, and they're quickly delivered so it requires no budget, and there is an unlimited resource. When the going gets tough, our relationship bank account must be rich with deposits, or it risks going bankrupt.

Positive Pollys never have to say, "Gee Fred, I'd like to respect you and acknowledge your castle construction and beautiful truck, but I am all out of respect and recognition for this quarter, so perhaps next one, I will be able to find a budget for it." Sounds funny, but the reality is that we are quite stingy when it comes to the showering of respect, compliments, acknowledgments, and other currencies that are a free, unlimited resource and have long-lasting impact with people.

What those positive Pollys might have to say is something inviting to approach a challenging conversation. Part of nurturing relationships is having important conversations as the need arises, and even though they might be flavored with tasty mud pie, or smell like something the cat left behind, they need to be worked through.

Assertive Play

Do you remember playing with friends in your early years and calling someone out on their behavior? "Hey, you just walked on my castle!" or "You've had the shovel for a long time and it's my turn!" Why did we lose that assertiveness? We've become uncomfortable having the challenging conversations that help keep behavior, structure, policies, procedures, safety, and fair play in line. Admit it, most people fear the conflict and discomfort of those types of chats, and so they avoid them. Unless of course they're keyboard warriors, firing nasty remarks while hiding behind the screen of email, text message, or social media. Let's face it, challenging conversations are just that—*challenging*—and many people just aren't up for the challenge.

There are times we need to nurture relationships by offering constructive feedback, questioning things that are happening, or calling people out on behavior versus commitments. We don't have to be managers or supervisors to need this skill. Difficult, challenging, crucial, or uncomfortable conversations can be an effective part of anyone's daily routine, and the only thing that's more difficult than having the conversation is not having it, or telling others about it rather than telling the person who can shift the behavior. HOLY SHIFT, that's gossip!

Luckily for us less-than-assertive people, there's a handy five-step process to help create a good mindset and approach to hold these types of conversations. With some prework, you will gain momentum to have the conversation because you'll decide if you're going to address the issue or not, why it matters, what your intention is, and what could happen if things go sideways. You'll see the process play out in the story below.

Kristie, a student nurse, was paired with Brian, a registered nurse, to job shadow and learn the day-to-day routines of the hospital setting. They were guided by Tammy, a facilitator from the nursing program whose job was to support the students transitioning from student nurse to independent practitioner within the framework of the university course structure and the hospital setting.

During her first shift on the floor, Kristie worked collaboratively with Brian to complete the head-to-toe assessment of their assigned patients. After the assessment, they were reviewing documentation forms, and she watched Brian check off an item in the tick charting that she hadn't noticed being assessed at the bedside. When charting the patient's respiratory assessment, Brian indicated that he listened to the patient's lungs and documented that they were clear. Kristie felt immediate distress as she did not observe Brian listening to the lungs. In her role as a student nurse in a new facility, she was unsure of how to proceed. She felt conflicted with the ethical framework she was taught and the falsifying of documentation that was being role modeled.

Kristie immediately sought out her instructor to share this experience, asked for support in how to proceed, and asked if she could be reassigned because she'd lost confidence in Brian's ability to set her up for success. In a conversation with Tammy, Kristie shared that she felt this practice was unethical, and that she was losing respect, doubting confidence in Brian, and questioning whether her work at the hospital—especially teamed up with Brian—was a good fit for her future.

Luckily for Kristie, Tammy facilitated a process to be able to approach the situation with some confidence and structure. Tammy's superpower is getting challenging conversations started, which for any workplace is a valuable tool. She sat with Kristie and took her through a series of questions so that she could reflect on what she saw happen, what she wanted to do about it, and why it mattered. Together they crafted the first statement to get the conversation started with Brian, as well as set a goal to have the conversation done by the end of the shift. Tammy was helping Kristie with professional accountability by providing conversational tools and tips and then giving her autonomy on the timing and setting of the conversation with one caveat: It had to occur before the shift ended and she had to report back to Tammy once it was done.

Her premeditated approach was well worth the time investment to create something that Kristie felt she could safely speak to. Although it was planned, and the first line was rehearsed, Kristie was still uncomfortable, which is absolutely normal. *Some* confidence is all we can expect at times when uncomfortable things need to be discussed. It took her some time to find the right moment and consider the variety of approaches she had explored with Tammy to find her "right" fit.

Kristie's decided approach was like extending the olive branch. She asked Brian if maybe they could return to listen to the patient's lungs together and could compare data. In presenting this moment for co-learning, Kristie effectively created a safe place for Brian to disclose his shortcomings. Brian admitted he did not listen and charted the lung sounds from the day before. He then shared this was common practice within the unit because there wasn't always time taken to check lungs daily, and staff would chart the data from the previous day. He later verbalized this was not the best practice and they did return to the patient to listen to the lungs, which were clear. Whew!

Several benefits were realized by Kristie, Brian, and the unit because of this experience and Kristie's willingness to speak up and step into a difficult conversation. Her confidence and competence to address practice issues strengthened, and she recognized how the role of being a student was hindering her desire to speak up. Kristie had also cleared many potential disasters, one being her respect for Brian. His honesty and willingness to receive the conversation was good sandbox play, and they built mutual respect and trust for their future working relationship.

As well, when Kristie reported back to Tammy on how the conversation went, word got back to the unit manager, who made mention of this important practice at the next morning's team huddle, reminding all staff to be checking lung sounds and charting them appropriately every time. Kristie's courage elevated the practice of those around her and prevented future moments of inaccurate documentation.

The value of Tammy's superpower, helping people get conversations started, followed through by Kristie, had a ripple effect through the entire unit. We all need to value our voice and speak up to the important conversations that will provide best practices, performance, peace, and profit.

Can you see how working through one challenging conversation could correct so many discrepancies that are not only important for employee performance and collaboration, but also for corporate missions and safety as well?

How would this story be different if there never was an approach to get a conversation started? What would the cost have been to not have the conversation? It is said that lack of communication is responsible for 70 percent of all sentinel events in health care.[6] These are human lives in jeopardy because of preventable mistakes, caused by either miscommunication, avoiding communication, and other symptoms like lack of trust, people swapping shifts or assignments, just to prevent the uncomfortable. Self-preservation is part of it too. People don't want to put themselves in situations where they may have to continue to speak to uncomfortable issues. It takes courage to do the right thing, especially when it doesn't feel good.

Five Steps to Challenging Conversations

The valuable process to prepare for and hold challenging conversations has five steps.

Step 1: Address It or Not

Decide whether you're going to address the issue or not. Is it a big deal? Can you let it go? Should you let it go? Sometimes we're so close to it (in it or emotional about it) that we need to take a step back from the issue and look at it from a different perspective. You may want to think about it from the professional standards or ethical framework of your profession. Is this against the integrity of who we are and what we stand for?

As well, you can do a *perception check* to make sure that you are decoding what you've observed accurately. A perception check is a message you can create to verify understanding of someone's behavior or words.

For example: If you didn't notice the nurse listening to the patient's lungs, did you miss something, or did he? Another example: If someone doesn't say hello or respond to yours, are they mad at you or just busy? We perceive things, and our perception isn't always accurate.

Step 2: Determine Your Intention

What is your intention or goal for the conversation? For example: to understand my colleague and maintain my own integrity.

Also, look through a lens of good intention from the other person's point of view. For example: Is it possible that he listened to the lungs when I wasn't looking? Giving the benefit of the doubt can shift the energy of a conversation toward the positive end goals you desire.

Step 3: Understand Why It Matters

Get to your WHY. Why does it matter to you? What value is causing you discomfort and, ultimately, driving you into action? Leveraging this *WHY power* can create a sense of obligation to speak up. For example: issues of patient safety.

Step 4: Imagine What Could Happen If It Doesn't Go as Planned

Communication is an art, not a science. Humans are complicated. Even the best intention and planning can go sideways. Sometimes asking yourself what's the worst-case scenario can empower you to stay the course. Hopefully it will. As a backup plan, you can always say, "Please give me some time to think this through, and let's meet again about it soon." A good old-fashioned time-out never hurt anyone. Don't use the excuse to exit the conversation for good. Make sure to honor your word of "meet again soon."

Step 5: Write Your Opening

Read it out loud. Soften if it feels abrasive.

When we are speaking, we should be using "I" statements, not "You" statements. Being "I" centered can't go too far wrong, because it's true for you, and doesn't blame the other person. Using an "I" statement and stating factual behavior is a great start. For example: "I feel conflicted between ethics and process. Can you help me understand better?"

Try having challenging conversations shortly after the situation arises. If your emotions are firing, perhaps give yourself a cooling-off period, but the best time to deal with challenges between yourself and anyone else is as soon as possible.

"It is noted by my colleagues," Tammy included, "that approaching difficult, challenging or crucial conversations results in a way better relationship in every case. You just have to trust that you can do it, and if you need some help use the five-step process to prepare."

Clear the Obstacles Daily

There was a two-year period in a personal relationship where my partner and I were both committed to cleaning up challenges and concerns between us as they arose. We talked often to get to the point of what I call "nothing between us," meaning that there was no resentment, no pent-up negative emotion, nothing accumulating, building, or boiling. We were more mature than those kids in the sandbox calling each other out, or stepping on castles, or not sharing, and the results were pure bliss! Fast-forward a couple of years and they weren't pure bliss anymore, and I realized that our values weren't aligned enough to make it long-term. A challenging, honest conversation sent us both in opposite directions. I don't think there are any failed relationship unless we're not learning the lessons. One of many lessons in that relationship was feeling the value of being completely connected with nothing in the way but a blank canvas for love and present-moment awareness. Nothing dangling over my head or pent up inside me. This is the reward for effectively working through both sides of giving and receiving challenging conversations.

Being uncomfortable for the time it takes to work through a conversation is quite empowering. As I've said, our comfort zones aren't all that comfortable anyway. Often, they're resting places for mediocrity, and pushing through them gives us a new sense of comfort that we've never known before. One great way to ensure that you and those you work with take care of their conversations is to be each other's accountability partners, holding each other responsible to have the talk necessary, and as soon as possible.

Nurturing is an action that will not only help those around you grow but will help you grow as well. Remember that respect, recognition, receiving, and remote all have the prefix *re*, which in the origin of our language means to "return to." By returning to these principles, you'll be taking action that nurtures relationships. Feedback can help you build better castles in the sand together, and when the need for a challenging conversation arises, pull out your five-step tool to prepare and then go for it!

Did you uncover any HOLY SHIFT opportunities to nurture relationships? Knowledge isn't power; action is power! Before moving on to the next chapter, write down your ideas to nurture relationships where you will be reminded often or download our worksheet companion.

6

Include Everyone

Everyone wants to feel part of the whole.

"Hey, that was my idea."

"That's my spot, I was here first."

"You took my sand."

"Who invited you, anyway?"

"Now children, the best way to build is to let everyone play," says Teacher . . . and that advice holds true today.

The synergy of a fully engaged, inclusive team is symbolic to throwing gas on the flame of your team's momentum, and the opposite, exclusion, is symbolic to extinguishing it with a bucket of water.

The issues created by exclusion are extensive. When people don't feel in on things, insecurity surfaces, and from there myriad problems can arise, which often result in some form of conflict. The goal of this chapter is to encourage peaceful workplace relationships by creating an inclusive approach to communication, cohesion, and conflict resolution. The hot topic of diversity, equity, and inclusion (DEI) is touched on later in the chapter with some astounding statistics that show a rapidly multiplying need for an inclusive culture in organizations across North America.

Over the past decade, my phone has rung steady with clients wanting to develop stronger relationships, better cohesion, and increased engagement and to turn the high cost of corporate conflict into peace, productivity, and profit. At the root of many of the cases I have mediated is a lack of people feeling included, or having the skills to resolve issues or work through their insecurities inclusively (with each other).

Exclusion Creates Conflict

I feel privileged to have had so many individuals share their inside secrets, sorrows, and stress about the real issues that have created conflict at work. Most of the issues could have been prevented or mitigated with a more inclusive strategy, and it's not just a top-down strategy that's needed. Everyone needs to dig in to create the inclusive culture that they're seeking—one that will collectively elevate their team dynamic to function for higher levels of success.

Below I have summarized a dozen issues that commonly create team dysfunction, disconnects, and frustration. Although problems on the surface cause a decision-maker to reach out to me for conflict resolution or team building, at the root of the issue is usually a lack of inclusion—people either being excluded or feeling excluded.

How many of these do you recognize in your workplace?

1. *People wanting to feel in on things*

    I worked with a small circle of health care managers who were not all connected. One felt excluded from the group. She had just returned from maternity leave, and her colleagues were meeting in offices with closed doors, socializing at lunch, and connecting over social media outside of the workplace. The conflict stemmed from something as simple as not being equally inclusive to all members on the team, and one person feeling left out. Like the seeds of a rose, a minor issue such as this one grows additional problems, similar to the petals of that flower. There were many situations stemming from that lack of inclusion that went on for almost a year before we nipped it in the bud with a mediation.

A survey of two hundred companies quizzed both managers and employees to determine the top three factors that contribute to employee morale. Managers and employees guessed opposing answers. Managers guessed high wages, job security, and promotions; employees surveyed confirmed appreciation, a feeling of being in on things, and an understanding attitude. People want to feel included in the building of ideas, to have a hand in decision-making, at least to be consulted, especially where their roles are affected.

2. *Bias toward each other, whether conscious or unconscious*
Social stereotypes about certain groups of people can be formed outside one's own conscious awareness. We all hold unconscious beliefs about various social and identity groups, and they stem from our tendency to organize social worlds by categorizing.[1] To become more aware of your unconscious bias, you can take a test such as the Implicit Association Test from Harvard.[2] When people become more aware of their bias, they are able to act with less bias, taking course-correcting actions and making decisions with the knowledge that they have their own biases. An example would be in the hiring decision to fill a position on an all-male executive team. The hiring manager might ask themselves if they are biased toward men, or if they should take another look with their bias in mind to see if they are being intentional, honest, and nonjudgmental in their choice to find the best candidate. Organizational consultant Lily Zheng eloquently addresses the bottom line of being bias-aware in her Quartz at Work article titled "What to Do with Your Implicit Bias": "Organizations are built by biased people working together to be self-aware, instead of objective people working to stave off their irrational biases. Our relationship with bias is one of healing and growth, rather than a 'fight.'"[3]

3. *Feeling of lack of fairness, equality*

Most organizations have policy and procedures. Many conflicts spark because they apply only to certain team members, while others get away with poor behavior without consequences. Inclusive means everyone gets equal and fair treatment, including consequences.

4. *Hiring process not followed*

Failure to follow consistent process creates turmoil. People feel excluded if they are overlooked for a promotion, especially when there is no follow-through conversation after hiring decisions are made. Employees are envious when a position comes available where the successor is predetermined before a fair competition. The continual struggle for women to gain high-level leadership positions continues with research showing that women are held back because they are encouraged to take accommodations, such as going part-time and shifting to internally facing roles, which derails their careers.[4]

5. *Assumptions made*

The grapevine runs rampant in organizations with a lack of communication from the top, and its toxic opportunity to breed misinformation ranks in the top issues that I experience in mediating workplace conflict and restoration cases. Remember playing "telephone" as a kid, where someone passes a message to someone, who passes it on and so on until the last person blurts out what they heard, and it has no resemblance to the original message? That happens with the workplace grapevine. The informal communication channel is fertile ground for rumors. People are curious, and if they aren't being included in communication from the top, they will seek details from each other.

6. *Employees going over their managers to report/complain*

When the hierarchy of the organizational chart is violated, conflict brews. No one likes to be undermined by their superior. If team members go over their manager or supervisor to the next level up, or to a different department's manager, the integrity of the organization's structure is comprised. We should allow for freedom to report situations where employees aren't getting traction from their direct supervisors, but how it's dealt with can make matters worse.

One of the largest workplace restorations that I worked with had over fifty disgruntled team members, their manager, and his senior manager. The price of that conflict included thousands of dollars for the restoration, which didn't come close to matching the cost of stress, low morale, lack of trust, and poor productivity that had plagued the department for months prior. The root of the problem was that the senior manager heard complaints from some team members about the manager, and rather than including the manager in on the conversations to resolve the issues, he did his own exclusive investigating, held team meetings to discuss the issues without the manager, and breached the organizational structure. Be mindful of who is involved and who should be included in conversations to rectify situations and hold true to the integrity of the organizational structure.

7. *Employees expecting managers to resolve conflict for them*
When teammates have conflict with each other, they may not have the skills to resolve it on their own and may need help from their manager or supervisor. Let's say John goes to his manager Lucy with raging anger about his colleague Phil, and expects Lucy to address Phil with the complaints. This is all too common. Lucy then tries to go to Phil, but she can't do John's listening for him, and she doesn't share the same emotion or experiences as John, so she is ill equipped without John and Phil in the same conversation at the same time to resolve the issues.

A manager well trained in conflict resolution would call a meeting to facilitate a conversation with John and Phil. "I hear that you are angry with Phil. Let's see if we can get him over here for a conversation about it." This will not only help guide the conversation but will empower each of them to go directly to each other in the future. If an issue recurs: "I understand you are upset with Phil. Did you speak with him about this?"

Attempting to resolve other people's conflicts rarely ends well and enables them to avoid practicing difficult conversations. It's like wanting someone to be more fit and doing their push-ups for them. Encourage people to gather and discuss issues in person, face-to-face on video, or by phone. Assist them by joining their conversation to mediate or guide it in a good way. You'll learn more mediation techniques in the next chapter.

8. *Team members talking about each other rather than to each other*
Gossip is talking negatively about someone. It breeds a lack of trust because when people experience a coworker who gossips about others, they wonder what would be said about them behind their back. It has a downward spiral effect on relationships and is popular as the root source of conflict among teams. I've never met someone who didn't admit they've gossiped in the workplace at some time or another.

The best way to avoid gossip is to include people into your conversations, or at least speak about them as if they were in the room.

People often ask me if there is a difference between gossip and venting. The term *venting* is generally used to describe blowing off steam when pressure builds up, or a release, and can be effective when negative emotions are running high. The problem is that most people "vent" about someone to someone else or, worse, to many others. That's gossip. Now the issue is off one's chest but onto others' and the person who has been "vented" about is still unaware of the specific issue that caused the venting in the first place. Rather than blowing hot air, why not tackle the issue itself? Vent to the person you're upset with. Hit it straight on and put it to rest immediately.

Venting to release emotion could be effective if you turn your energy from blaming to a learning conversation about yourself. For example: "She did this and that and it put me in a real predicament" is more like gossip than "I felt like I was put in a real predicament when she did this and that." The latter takes responsibility for one's own feelings and begins the responsibility and accountability to talk out loud to reach a potential solution.

Venting can be healthy, but when people start making assumptions or accusations about a coworker's intent rather than sticking to facts, the conversation is moving into gossip. When comments become about a person's character rather than their specific behavior, it becomes problematic. For example: "She doesn't let me finish speaking before she cuts me off" is a specific behavior where "She is so rude" is painting someone's character with a negative brush. Gossip tends to become habit, and when negative comments about someone continue to be the topic without a solution-focused approach, the destructive behavior takes a toll on the listener.

In my experience with workplace conflict, there is often a "go-to" person who will listen to gossip or venting and gain a sense of value from their role as "office counselor." Once they realize the price they're paying to receive the burdens of others, they want a HOLY SHIFT. They want to stop enabling gossip and start holding people accountable to create the workplace environment where everyone can thrive. The office "go-to" might shift behavior by stating, "I understand you feel that she interrupts you. Let's discuss ways to approach the conversation with her." Another option I've witnessed many times is the wanna-be reformed office "go-to" tells all their peers that they no longer want the role or title because the cost of stress and negativity is devastating them. That's my favorite moment! I love seeing people admit how they've contributed to dysfunctional team dynamics, choose something healthier for themselves, and verbalize it with confidence to initiate a new way of being. So powerful!

Gossip is a sign of a toxic work environment where politics and personalities get more attention than the tasks needing to be completed.[5] Liane Davey, author of *The Good Fight* and *You First*, suggests in a *Harvard Business Review* article[6] that we give a frustrated teammate a chance to close the door and vent, then shift into a more constructive conversation about how to rectify their situation, or seek help from someone who can remedy the problem before the toxicity affects the entire team.

9. *Lack of trust in leadership*

Lack of trust in leadership has been the source of quite a few workplace issues. There are often questions about what leadership is doing in all those closed-door meetings. When people are not included in the whole conversation, they doubt the decisions made by their leaders because they don't see the big picture. Although confidentiality is important for certain information, it's a balancing act of what to say, what not to say, and to whom. Every organization is different, but the more information that can be shared, the more included a team member will feel.

High-level leaders on the organizational structure are role models who people look up to. If there is confidential information shared, or negative comments about other people spoken by them, a culture of low trust is created.

When executives or managers are against each other, their respective departmental teams know it, and they are usually talking about it. Trust can erode between entire departments very quickly.

Turnover in high positions can create a lack of trust, especially if the loss of a great leader is mourned by the team, or a rogue leader has left an unsafe legacy behind. Trust is a marathon, not a sprint. Be inclusive to begin to regain trust with people.

10. *Lack of clarity in roles, goals, and vision*

As we recover from the pandemic and regain our balance of people to roles, there is lack of clarity as to who is doing what, with whom. The "cabinet shuffle" of team members can leave a very confused workforce, where no one is clear on where they fit in to the new vision of the organization. Clarity of the big picture will help people understand where they fit in the overall picture.

11. *Disconnected teams*

Many are playing in a virtual sandbox with their own shovel and pail but are isolated from the group and sitting inside their own headspace. They're not sure who else is doing what, how they fit in, compare, compete, or collaborate. Whether in person, remote, or hybrid, the shifting sands of change have turned many routines upside down and disconnect has replaced the inclusive function that was known in the past.

12. *Interpersonal conflict*

There are many human differences in a diverse workplace including personality styles, which often plague organizations because people expect others to be like them, rather than accept them as being different. The best workplace has every personality style represented so that the synergy of strengths can provide the widest range of skill and ability. The bottom line of most personality style modalities is that treating others as THEY want to be treated includes them effectively into conversations, decisions, and ways of socializing and working together.

The antidote to this bouquet of a dozen issues that create conflict is to create an inclusive environment . . . most of which is an inside job. If each person could start by taking inventory of issues they recognize as their behavior, and can do something to be more inclusive, there would be less team conflict, more peace, greater productivity, less stress, and more money to put to better use. Go back and read the list again to find ways that you might find your nuggets of truth, to create a more inclusive environment. Maybe something will land on your list of HOLY SHIFT notes for future action.

Create an Inclusive Environment

Creating an inclusive environment in your workplace sandbox is very valuable on just about as many fronts as there are multifaceted people in it.

An inclusive mindset can smooth many differences. For example, intergenerational workplace challenges are based on different ages, life experiences, values, and skill sets. Regardless of whether we are Boomers or Gen X, Y, or Z, at the end of the day, we all want the same thing. We want the best pay for the least amount of time invested, the most time off possible (work-life balance), and to make a difference, be acknowledged, and fit into a positive and collaborative workplace culture. I think that rings true for all people, regardless of their grouping. Thinking about the generational gaps with your inclusivity hat on, you might establish a mentor program to match senior and junior people together to share knowledge and skills. Each has value to contribute. Encourage younger generations to be part of decision-making by inviting them to sit on committees where they can gain a sense of being included.

Inclusion with a Circle Approach

Inclusion means working together. The conceptual model of our Sandbox System is a round circle inside the (sand)box, to signify the unity of the team that is required despite the multifaceted dynamics.

In my approach to workplace mediations and restorations, I use the circle format to include everyone and create unity. Learned from very special Indigenous people, this method removes barriers like boardroom tables or desks from between the participants and allows them to connect face-to-face for authentic conversations. When skillfully led and facilitated, this inclusion-based format has always provided great results of peace and new commitments, which creates team engagement and saves corporations millions of dollars.

I've sat in circles as small as two plus myself, and as big as fifty or sixty people from an entire department. This process begins with some commitments to honesty, confidentiality, and acceptance. The intention is to share honestly with one another, to understand each other, and to relieve stress and resentment in exchange for some new commitments to work better together. It's transformational, and I feel so grateful to watch the process unravel before my eyes.

When we can include everyone in a transparent conversation, hear honest feedback, and speak to and listen to each other respectfully and inclusively, we become ready for the next stages of resolution, which is to make new commitments together. That is the basis of mediation, which is a facilitated dialogue where two or more parties find solutions better than either one of them could have come up with on their own.

Inclusion is something to be integrated into everything that we do—woven into how we operate, communicate and interact, run meetings, delegate assignments, and implement policy. It's not an additional task that we have to put on top of our duties, rather, a fundamental way of thinking and being that we are all in this together.

The skills required to foster inclusivity include curiosity, empathy, listening, communication, feedback, and a peripheral vision that sees all 360 degrees of the circle of your work team.

Here's a story of a great coach and consultant who has inspired many teams with the skills that create inclusivity in work teams.

Tapping Their Genius

Mike Campigotto has enjoyed a long career as a management consultant. A lunch with this legend in my hometown of North Bay, Ontario, enlightened me further on two of the top issues he found held people back from playing nice, and he shared two powerful questions he encourages teams to ask to expand their thinking.

Far from inclusion, people often draw a line in the sand to protect their "territory"—meaning their own position, level of control, level of authority, or profile within the organization. There's a resistance to the detriment of growth of the company or the individuals, and that's when "selfish" isn't good. There's a problem with collaboration and teamwork that is fundamentally based in a resistance to expose one's "territory" to change.

What if we could change the labels of jobs and roles to tools and territory?

To solve this and many other problems over the course of his career, Mike uses the question, "How might we . . . ?" The first time I heard this question working with Mike on a project, I realized that it shifted gears in my head to find a solution. I never forgot it. Asking,

"How might we" as a conversation starter with a team to problem solve gets people thinking outside their traditional ways of thinking. The question itself is like a doorway to the possible, where people may have thought before about limitations or restrictions.

To dig even deeper, a second question could be, "How might we do it now if there were no restrictions or limitations?" This always gets a new answer. It's virtually applicable in every situation, and it gets people involved in cocreating the ideas that they themselves will buy into (because people love to feel in on things) and more committed to the application of their own ideas. It's a brilliant question that greases the wheels of the next step for incremental change or a broad, sweeping change.

"Once you have that open door to thinking about how to tackle the problem, together with the 'how might we,' they can shift limits of their imagination and take apart assumptions and rules in their head. These rules in their head haven't been validated or stated, they've just been assumed, and seemed logical until now, where they don't apply. Without rules in our head, the creativity tap opens in full force."

"How might we" has helped Mike and his team create a successful start-up. SafeSight is an innovations company that develops and offers cutting-edge solutions for the mining industry, with over seven innovations, flying drones underground to map and model in 3D, increasing the safety of personnel while collecting real-time data.

Imagine what you could cocreate as a team with the question "How might we . . . ?"

Collaboration across Two Sandboxes

About a year after I rebranded my company's main product to PLAY NICE in the Sandbox with Penny Tremblay, I was searching Amazon on the topic and found an author, speaker, and trainer similar to me, who had . . . "Hey wait a minute . . . that was my idea" . . . a book titled *Play Nice in Your Sandbox at Work.* I ordered it immediately, and secretly hoped that he never noticed that I had created the same brand as his book title. Within a couple of weeks, I received a copy with a handwritten note from the author.

"Penny, I am honored that you would have an interest in my book. From the looks of your website, you are who I hope to be when I 'grow up.' I am also happy to be playing in a different, but in some ways similar, sandbox with you. If you see possibilities for joint ventures for mutual benefit, please know that I am totally open to having that discussion. For now, Ron Price." I was so impressed!

I took a photo of myself holding his book and sent him a card with the photo printed inside, along with a copy of my book *Give and Be Rich*.[7] A collaboration felt incredible ... better than an evil eye on my competition.

Over time, Ron and I stayed in touch, and he referred me to other leaders in our same industry of mediation and training for workplace harmony. I wanted to include him in this book, and my first request was another one for collaboration. "You know, Ron, how your book is formatted with P.L.A.Y. N.I.C.E. as an acronym for lessons?" I said early in the interview. "Well, I want to run the same theme through my book with different ideas for what the letters in the acronym mean, and I wanted to ask you how you felt about that first." Ron was surprised and honest with me. He said "Penny, it's a big world and I'll be honest, my first thinking is 'Hey, that's mine,' but that's *stinkin' thinkin'*, and I am interested in working collaboratively."

Ron and I spent a few moments hashing out the possibilities of referring each other as speakers and trainers to clients, and we were already sharing and bouncing ideas off each other. Over the course of the interview, we gave each other many great ideas and strategies, encouraging them to be used for the benefit of each other's programs.

I learned a long time ago from Jack Canfield that amateurs compete, but experts collaborate. Ron made me laugh out loud when he said, "Wouldn't it be something if the two PLAY NICE in the sandbox people couldn't get along?" Not everyone in your sandbox will be such a joy to play with, but an approach that you can try when seeking collaboration is to ask for it. Not take it without asking or demand it, but ask about the possibility of working together, and let the other person take a step forward to you. Collaboration wins over competition every time.

A Culture of Candor at Pixar

For people to be transparent, they have to feel psychological safety to express themselves. In his book *Creativity, Inc.*, Ed Catmull,[8] co-founder of the multibillion-dollar company Pixar Animation, writes about creating a culture of candor, where people are encouraged to be "necessarily honest" with each other.

Candor means "open and honest in expressions, frankness, honesty, truthfulness, forthrightness"; its origin comes from the Latin meaning "whiteness," which, when you really think about that, means "pure." Pure conversation wouldn't have to be colored with anything other than what it is and why it's important that nothing is left unspoken.

A culture of candor must come from the top leaders in the organization, or people won't feel safe to speak openly and honestly, because leaders get the behavior that they reward. If someone speaks up or out, and it's perceived as a negative experience or they're penalized, it won't happen again. A subversive culture can start a revolution within, whereas a culture of candor starts honesty and truthfulness.

This is where good sandbox training comes in, and a healthy sandbox factor of employees can shift an organization into a culture of candor. People need to learn how to give and receive criticism or constructive feedback from the foundation of good intention, of building people up rather than tearing them down.

Even when people are resistant, the path through an open and honest dialogue removes assumptions and misconceptions about what is going on, and the intention behind it.

Including Remote Workers

Distance erodes trust. Remote workers feel *out of sight, out of mind.* The inclusion efforts required for those not physically in the workplace need to be amplified to have the same impact as those who are in person as expressed in the previous chapter, under the heading "Retain Remote Workers with Respect."

Dig into Diversity

Today's workplaces are more multifaceted than ever.[9] We have multiple generations, multiple cultures, multiple personality styles, multiple genders, different morals, and different values, but so what? Why do we seek "same" in a workplace culture with such differences? The workplace sandbox is diverse. Diversity is variety, and variety is the spice of life!

The more accepting and nonbiased we are becoming as a society, the more diverse we want to become in the workplace. Minorities will be the source of all growth in youth and working-age population as far into the future as we can see. The United States will become "minority white" in 2045, according to census projections.[10] In 2019, most new hires were people of color.[11] By the year 2060, it is estimated that 43.6 percent of the US population will be white.[12] The Latinx population will take up more than 20 percent of the workforce by 2028, with almost half being women (Latinas),[13] and an increasing number of individuals identify as LGBT at an average of 4.5 percent per state, with younger generations more likely to self-identify.[14]

Diversity, Equity, and Inclusion Defined

Diversity, equity, and inclusion (DEI) is a very popular term that describes programs and policies to promote the representation and participation of different groups of people including people of different ages, races and ethnicities, abilities, genders, religions, cultures, and sexual orientations.

The pandemic has amplified a preexisting global workforce, yet we've paid lip service to DEI for decades, and are still making only minimal progress.[15]

Each letter in the DEI acronym supports a different aspect of support.[16]

Diversity is the presence of differences that may include race, gender, religion, sexual orientation, ethnicity, nationality, socioeconomic status, language, (dis)ability, age, religious commitment, or political perspective. Populations that have been—and remain—underrepresented among practitioners in the field and marginalized in the broader society.

Equity is promoting justice, impartiality, and fairness within the procedures, processes, and distribution of resources by institutions or systems. Tackling equity issues requires an understanding of the root causes of outcome disparities within our society.

Inclusion is an outcome to ensure those who are diverse actually feel and/or are welcomed. Inclusion outcomes are met when you, your institution, and your program are truly inviting to all, to a degree where diverse individuals can participate fully in the decision-making processes and development opportunities within an organization or group.[17]

Inclusion Is Like Clay

Cohesion is a common goal of a team, defined as the action of forming a united whole. In science terms, cohesion is formed by the electrical attraction of molecules.

Sand on its own is not cohesive. It doesn't stick together because of its chemical composition. The essence of sand is impermanence, because it loses form and shape, which inspires our sensory brain to continue to build. Inclusion is like the clay that must be added to the sand to create cohesion. We model with clay, create what we want, and it hardens to remain in form. Consider thinking and acting inclusively at work to be synonymous with adding clay to your sandbox. Ordinary sand needs that extra element of clay to be extraordinary.

Remember the little army soldiers that we played with in the sand? If one fell outside the sandbox, children would pick it up and add it to their army, knowing that there is strength in numbers, or that no one would want to be alienated outside the box.

By weaving inclusivity into our daily efforts, we create a culture of candor that can prevent or mitigate conflict and the associated costs to the people and companies they represent. When people feel in on things, they engage, and they stay more committed to change than when they feel excluded.

What would it take to be the spark that attracts others to your work team and have them stay?

7

Challenge Conflict

Healthy teams learn to embrace it.

EVEN WHEN YOU'RE NURTURING AND INCLUDING OTHERS, SOME people are like cats on the edge of your sandbox just waiting to dig in and bury a turd.

> *Conflict is inevitable. Damaged relationships are optional.* —Ron Price

Do you avoid conflict?

Digging in to challenge conflict is not as difficult as people might think, but most people fear conflict and try to avoid it. Conflict has a negative connotation, like a challenging win/lose idea that we must fight through. The reality is, there's only one way through conflict, and that is **through it**. You can't go over it or under it or around it, you must go through the fire, but you'll burn off things that just aren't worth carrying around anymore.

In a conversation with author, psychotherapist, and YouTube influencer Lise Leblanc, she admitted that unpacking her suitcase of old stories played a major factor in her ability to succeed with a second authoritarian boss, much like the first.

I was twenty-eight years old when I landed my first management job. It was a great opportunity, and I was very excited, but there was a downside: the executive director was perceived as a bully. The employees were in the process of bringing a union in and there was an "us against them" mentality between staff and management. In addition, the fifteen-person management team had created a cesspool of gossip and negativity. We thought we were supporting each other. We called it "venting." The reality was, we were depleting each other's energy by getting each other more enrolled in this victim story. None of us had the tools, strategies, or skills to show up to this situation in a more positive and productive way. So instead, we continued going from office to office, recounting all the terrible things she was doing. Then we brought the same stories home. We were in a complete state of dysfunction with all of us thinking our boss was the problem. Our next step was to get the board of directors involved in hopes that they could fix her. It got even worse from that point on.

Unfortunately, we had all bought into the story that she was the problem and that we couldn't do anything about it, other than undermine her, gossip about her, and basically bully her in return. This had become a collective story that we were all feeding into. We were creating a workplace culture that was very toxic and this toxicity took its toll. This situation coupled with some home/life issues, including the loss of my grandfather, completing my master's degree, and caring for my young children and my grandmother who had Alzheimer's disease, led me to a breaking point. Fortunately, this breakdown turned into a breakthrough as it led me to start unpacking my suitcase, which had become too heavy to carry. Here is one of the surprises I discovered in my suitcase. . . .

Although my boss was just a bit over five feet tall, I felt very intimidated by her from the moment I met her. I didn't know it at the time, but her stern eyes subconsciously reminded me of my grade three teacher who seemed to take pleasure in humiliating me in front of the rest of the class. When I heard my boss's quick, heavy footsteps coming down the hallway, I would get nervous, I would start wondering whether she was coming to my office and worrying about whether I'd done something wrong. Most of the time she wasn't coming to see me, but on those occasions when she did come to my office, by the time she got there, I was already shut down emotionally. As I unpacked my suitcase, I came to realize that subconsciously her heavy footsteps reminded me of my mother's quick, heavy footsteps when she was flying into my room in a rage when I was just a little girl. The fear response I was having had little to do with my boss—I was simply superimposing a fear I'd had of authority figures onto her. It got to a point where I felt "stressed" anytime my boss was around. If I pulled into the parking lot and saw her vehicle was not there, I would breathe a huge sigh of relief. If her car was there, I immediately got uptight and justified my fear by making her the "bully." Here I was thinking it was all her, when in truth, it was the unresolved pain from my past that was affecting me. I truly had no idea that I was shifting back and forth from a relatively mature adult to a hurt and scared child anytime I was triggered by my boss's behavior. I was seeing her through the eyes of the unhealed child within, and sadly these painful childhood experiences were standing in the way of me showing up as a healthy and productive woman in my workplace. Once I connected these dots, I made a commitment to dive into the deep work of healing. During my healing process, I worked with a therapist who helped me uncover what my ego was filtering, including core beliefs, blind spots, and coping mechanisms that were no longer serving me. The work was well worth the effort because the irony here is that after two years of healing work, I took a new job and quickly realized I was entering a very similar territory with a very similar workplace culture and a boss who had a similar management style. However, I was showing up differently. I had new tools to communicate as a responsible adult. I was coming in with the intention and commitment to creating positive and productive workplace relationships with coworkers <u>and</u> my boss with whom I developed a healthy, respectful, and mutually supportive relationship. I no longer participated in gossip. Instead of worrying what everyone else was up to, I concerned myself with my own integrity and with taking responsibility for the way I was showing up to create a healthy and positive workplace.

As you can see from Lise's story, a very similar situation turned out very differently once she resolved her painful experiences from the past. She was no longer perceiving and interpreting the world through the eyes of the unhealed child within. In other words, her past was what needed resolve, so that she could show up differently to the challenges in the workplace.

When you continue carrying around your old hurts and resentments from the past, they will keep showing up in different ways in your life. Until you unpack this stuff, you will keep responding in the same old ways and thinking that someone else is to blame for your recurrent challenges. This is why much of dealing with conflict is an inside job, and as such, it is not what happens to you but rather how you resolve it that counts.

Resolving Conflict Starts Within

People don't always want to dig deep into the old wounds that they've got locked up inside. The reality is, they don't have to, but there's a cost to live with baggage in your suitcase, and a cost to unpack it. Either way there's a cost, so the better question is, what do you want? What kind of freedom, and peace, and present-moment awareness and quality of life do you seek? Then, decide to pay that price, and do the inner work. If you see things about yourself or your past that you can't deal with alone, then reach out for help. Seek therapy. Find a circle of friends or a close confidant who will call you out on the patterns that you're blind to.

There's more stress in **not** dealing with the conflict than there is once you've begun the process. Some perceive that living with conflict or approaching challenging conversations will upset themselves and others, but it's the opposite. Working through conflict is where the calm begins.

How long do you want to stay in the storm? The only thing worse than being in conflict for two months, two weeks, or two days is one more day.

The Knotted Rope

I use a unique prop in my education programs to symbolize team member entanglements. It's a large knot of different-color and different-size ropes all tangled up together. I relate it to workplace conflict with the notion that everyone owns a part of the mess, and if each person could just reach in and take out their piece, own it by honestly admitting what they have contributed to the conflict, and commit to doing better, there would be nothing left but peace. The prop has become an impactful metaphor and symbol that encourages people to untangle the mess by taking responsibility for what is theirs, rather than blaming others.

We need to understand what's ours and what's not ours. The beauty of getting to know what's yours is that you'll be clear on your responsibility and what you need to act on or shift. The rest isn't yours, and you have no control over changing other people. If you spend your energy fixing yourself, you'll be miles ahead in your relationship potential, and you will have fewer loose ends for others to get entangled with.

Know What's Yours

This became very clear to me one day a few years back when I moved into a new home and was unpacking my jewelry. I came across two of my favorite chains that were knotted together in a complex mess. One was my fine long silver necklace that I wore all the time with different pendants, and the other was a gold chain given to me by my parents when I made the sacrament of confirmation in our Catholic faith as a young teenager. I loved and wore these two pieces often, and I was absolutely devastated to see them tangled into what seemed like an impossible resolution.

I decided to tackle the issue. It took me a long time of very concentrated, steady-handed work, during which time I had to get brighter lights and some tools to pick at the knots. I got thinking about how symbolic this was to conflict between people. In this state of entanglement, the chains were completely dysfunctional, similar to the dysfunction of a work team, their performance and productivity, when they're stifled and stagnated by conflict.

I realized that to untangle the knots, I really had to see them, and the brighter light helped shine an awareness of the position of each of them and their complicated entanglement. The brighter light was a symbol of awareness and willingness to see the knots, which people aren't always willing to look at. The light also made the hues of metal very distinct, which helped me realize what was gold and what was silver. Reflecting on the similarities of life, I thought of how there are things that are distinctly mine, and things that are not mine at all; and knowing what belongs to whom is an important first step in unwinding the pieces, because you can only deal with your own stuff, and as much as you'd like to deal with others' stuff, control it or influence it, that part is up to them.

I got to a point where I couldn't get one last knot undone. It was beyond my capabilities, and so I had to take it to a professional jeweler. I may have been able to use greater force, but I didn't want to break the fragile chains while trying, so I reached out for help. The next day I picked up two separate chains that were cleaned and ready for new life, all for under ten bucks. This was so symbolic to people, sometimes needing to reach out to a third party, a neutral person, a mediator like myself, or a counselor or specialist to help them resolve some of those "harder to untangle" knots in their conflicts with other people without using force that could break fragile relationships altogether.

From Blame to Buttons

This is taking responsibility for challenging conflict. When someone pushes your button(s), just know that you have a button to push, and it's yours and you get to work through it, hopefully with the intention to get rid of your own button, rather than expecting someone else to shift their behavior to accommodate your button.

It's human nature to blame other people for the fact that we can't be, do, or have whatever we want, or that we're feeling slighted or frustrated or just not good enough. When conflict plagues us, we tend to want to find fault in the other person and point the blame. If you take your pointing finger and point it at someone, you'll find three of your own fingers are pointing back at you. Take the time to see what's yours, feel it, honor it, write about it in your journal, talk about it with a trusted friend, or get professional help. Let other people have what's theirs. It will make you crazy to try to change anyone, and besides, it's not your job. "Not your monkey, not your circus," my lovely assistant Monica says. When you're clear and honest about what's yours, you only have half the work to do, but it's the only half that you have control and power to shift, so that's where you need to spend your time and effort.

Hundreds of times I've sat with office teams who wanted greater team cohesion, or a new culture, and I helped them see their own pieces of the knotted entanglements of conflict, and own it, and vulnerably admit it, "This is mine." That vulnerability and humility sets people free from their own binds, and others are very respectful to these intimate behaviors.

There are times when human entanglements are more complicated and complex, and they require a third party to help resolve the issues. I highly recommend the assistance of experts who can help you move through relationship snags effectively and efficiently. When our car needs maintenance, we take it in for service. When our bones are broken, we go to the hospital. When our plumbing isn't flowing, we call a plumber (well, at least I do). When we're struggling with relationships, we should be willing to reach out for help, because people matter, and broken relationships are not only costly with money, but they're emotionally exhausting and cause a great deal of stress and heartache. Don't push too hard to break something as fragile as an important relationship before reaching out for help.

The Three-Bite Rule

Getting along with people doesn't always click in the first interaction. Sometimes it takes a few attempts or, shall I say, a few bites.

"Take three bites. If you don't like it, you don't have to eat anymore." This was a rule I had for my young children when I wanted them to try new foods, and the same concept works for business relationships, and personal ones too.

I have two children, seventeen months apart. Back in their preschool years, I found myself catering to each of their likes and dislikes for meals or arguing with them to eat food that they didn't want or like. It was time-consuming and stressful. I felt like a short-order cook in a restaurant, but no one ever paid their bill or even left a tip. Trying to please everyone's palate was exhausting my patience and I assumed there was a better way, so I spoke with my friend Mitch who fed three kids about the same ages as mine. She put me onto her *three-bite rule*, and I made it official with an announcement.

"I'll only be cooking one meal for the family; you'll be served a little bit of everything onto your plate, and you must take at least three honest bites to give it a good try. If you don't like it, you don't have to eat any more. Next time I'm serving the same food, you'll get some on your plate and you can try three bites again. Over time you may learn to like it." I posted a "like list" where each of the kids were able to add new foods they liked, and I made a big deal out of recognizing and praising them for their growing list.

Once the rule was in place, I enforced it gently because I wanted the kids to enjoy coming to the table for family meals and not be stressed about it. The biggest challenge was getting everyone at the table to play by the rules. It took me a week to catch on that my picky eater's bites were being eaten for him by his father when I wasn't looking. I realize that their father was trying to help with good intentions, but it was undermining the new program and enabling the old behavior. We talked about it privately and I asked him to let the kids eat their own bites. He obliged and the kids were trying, but it wasn't without icky faces or unpleasant clues of distaste, but we stuck with it.

Within the next few weeks the three-bite rule was working well, little people were expanding their "like list" of foods, and I was satiated knowing that my meal prep was efficient, my kids were being nourished, and mealtime was more enjoyable.

I know we're not eating our teammates or customers, but we're probably trying to like them, accept them, or just play nice in the business sandbox, and that might take a few attempts. Not everyone is tasty at first. Some people's personalities seem too sweet, too sour, or downright tough or bitter!

Maybe you've reached out to someone with an open appetite, and they bit your head off. (Just a figure of speech—we should never tolerate physical violence.) That's only one bite, right? What if you could have an unwritten three-bite rule for people who aren't receptive to your approach, and you could keep on trying? A second attempt might leave a different taste in your mouth. Give them the benefit of the doubt and try a third pursuit if the first two didn't land in a good way or weren't received with open arms.

Rather than deciding on the first bite, whether it's your approach or someone's crusty response, that you don't have an appetite for a working relationship with them, keep on sampling the possibility that you're going to develop a pleasant relationship over time. Find other opportunities to make relationships work together and be open to new flavors. Don't let one attempt at what could be a good working relationship leave a bad taste in your mouth. It may be different from your typical ways of being or doing, but it's not necessarily wrong or bad, it's just different. Different isn't all that different after you've experienced it many times.

Need proof of how this rule can work for you? Make a list of five things you eat now that you didn't like when you were five. (Beer and wine don't count.) Over time, we appreciate variety and diversity. Now think about the people you look up to because they're good at getting along with others. They've probably taken more than one bite (attempt to like the person[s]) before deciding that they're no good with people, or that it's too risky to try and try again. The more we try, the more we add skills and effort over the years with different people, which helps us learn to play nice in the adult sandboxes.

I recall watching a short video clip of a couple celebrating their seventy-fifth wedding anniversary. Someone asked the woman what her secret was to being married that long. I'll never forget her answer. "In our day, if something was broken, we fixed it, we didn't just throw it in the garbage." What if we could help people stay committed to working out relationship challenges rather than throwing them in the garbage . . . leaving their employment, filing lawsuits, filing short- or long-term insurance claims, or divorcing or never speaking to someone who matters in their life? Seventy-five years together, wow, that's a lot of bites!

Taking three bites for making relationships work exercises our tolerance muscles. I don't know where those are in the body, but I know that they are weak until worked, and gain strength as we tolerate different people, personality styles, ethnicities, generational differences, and so much of the diversity that we find in business today.

I hope the three-bite rule will encourage you to find a little bit more appetite for getting past a distasteful experience. My parents taught me that time heals. When our emotions calm down, we might be in a better position to try another bite, a gentle bite, with intention to like the food, and add another rich flavor to our like list.

Ending Unhealthy Relationships

Taking three bites to make relationships work, and then another three bites the next time we have a chance to try it again, gives us a frame of mind that we need to keep on extending the olive branch when relations are rocky; but what about knowing when to end a relationship that is unhealthy? Workplaces and personal relationships can be fertile grounds for verbal abuse.

PLAY NICE in the sandbox doesn't mean accepting abuse. Knowing what verbal abuse is, sounds like, or feels like is an important beginning to dealing with it. Here are some general characteristics.

Verbal abuse is hurtful and often denied by the victim because it's discounted or not validated by the abuser, so part of the hurt is confusion. It attacks one's nature because the victim believes that there's something wrong with their abilities or feelings. It may be overt (blaming and accusatory) or covert (brainwashing, hidden aggression), both of which are attempts at control. It may be voiced in a sincere way, leading the victim to believe there is good intention behind the malice, and is manipulating and controlling because the victim may not realize that they're being controlled.

Verbal abuse is insidious (disrespects the victim to diminish esteem and confidence) and unpredictable because the victim doesn't expect it or understand why it occurs or how to prevent it. The issue is the abuse, rather than a real conflict to resolve or find closure with. It sends a double message because the abuser's words and feelings are incongruent. They say they're peaceful, but their behavior seems angry or irritable and it often escalates, increasing in intensity, frequency, and variety. What might seem like jokes in the beginning are put-downs that turn to more verbal abuse, and often physical abuse.[1]

Abuse is a heavy topic, but it's worth understanding the characteristics of an unhealthy relationship where verbal abuse is involved. Here are a few things you can do about it with some examples of what to say:

- Start setting your boundaries verbally. *"I will not accept being put down with your jokes."*
- Stay in the present, not the past or future, and speak up immediately to angry or disparaging remarks directed at you. *"Stop the remarks."*
- Be aware that you can leave any abusive situation. You're a free citizen, and you never have to stay where you don't feel safe.
- Be solution based in your request for your needs to be met. *"I need you to offer feedback in a more respectful way / more gentle tone."*
- Get professional support. Report this to a supervisor, a manager, human resources, or someone you feel safe with.

We teach people how to treat us. Taking three bites to make relationships work is not thirty bites. As Kenny Rogers said, "You gotta know when to hold 'em, know when to fold 'em." Don't be afraid to set boundaries for yourself of what you will and won't accept from others who aren't adapting to your attempts to get along. Let people know that you're interested in a respectful relationship and that when they're ready to meet you in that place, your door is open. Standing up and setting your own limits to what you will and won't stand for is empowering, and it's your right. Taking three more bites isn't necessarily going to help all relationships get to collaboration and respect, so know your cues, characteristics, and cures for staying healthy among relationship challenges. Sometimes the taste of too bitter will never get sweet, and we can't change others, only how they affect us. Abuse is hurtful to the spirit, but with knowledge, awareness, and support, we can leverage the emotional workout and loss of something that's not functional to reach a new level of freedom.

Embrace Conflict Within

There's a healthy side of conflict. When we move through challenges that arise, or clean up old stuff when it's discovered, we become stronger and more confident, yet lighter in our burdens and free from the ties of our past.

When we can let go—we grow.

Moving through conflict doesn't always feel positive or good, but life isn't about always just feeling good—it's about doing the right things. Positive thinking was the rage for years, but let's get real here. Negative stuff happens. We get hurt. We come up on hurdles and obstacles regularly, and our authentic self doesn't feel positive; it feels heavy and depressing. The only way to get through something is to go through it. Not around it, over it, or under it. Through it. What's right for your spirit, your body, and your mind isn't always positive. But there are multiple perspectives to look at things, and just by HOLY SHIFTING your view on a challenging situation you could help find the good. There is usually a bless in the mess. You won't always have to be feeling positive about a situation or set of circumstances to find peace with it. Just find peace in doing the right thing.

The best cure for conflict is not just thinking positive, or pushing things down, or numbing them out with drugs, alcohol, or other addictive substances or activities. The best cure is more of the same. Like the world of homeopathy, where like cures like, we need to embrace conflict.

Embrace Team Conflict

Conflict and combat are so linked in our thought process, team members see conflict as dysfunctional and counterproductive. Leaders perceive team conflict as a source of lost productivity and opportunities, something that creates a lack of inspiration and cohesiveness among employees. Without embracing conflict for the opportunity that it presents, both of these perceptions are correct.

In *The Beauty of Conflict: Harnessing Your Team's Competitive Advantage*, authors CrisMarie Campbell and Susan Clarke identify opportunities to turn conflict into the juice that powers a team, because in a sandstorm of conflict, vision, opinion, and passion can come together to create a perfect storm for creativity and innovation. It all starts with a willingness to embrace conflict and not sweep it under the carpet in avoidance.[2]

Once you're aware and ready to loosen your tight grip on the issues (new and old) that aggravate, they can be seen as opportunities, not threats. You'll find yourself just as scared as you did years ago, but you'll embrace them with more courage and intention to see them for what they really are, and why they're there. Letting go or detaching can take a long time, and a great deal of self-cultivation, agitation, and aggravation before all those weeds and seeds of the past are neutralized. Meanwhile, give yourself credit for trying.

Agitation—the Magic Bullet

One day I was dressed in my favorite white business suit, ready to leave my home and rock the stage for a local speaking engagement. To nourish myself on the drive into town, I decided to make a refreshing blueberry smoothie. I made it just as I usually do, with local frozen blueberries that I'd picked just weeks before, a banana, and my favorite pure orange juice, blended in my Magic Bullet smoothie cup blender. My mouth was watering just waiting for the first cold, sweet taste, and my tummy was ready for what it knows so well to be the coolest nutrition boost, liquid food, no muss no fuss breakfast.

I stopped the blender, unhooked the cup, turned it right side up, and twisted the blender blade off the top of the smoothie glass. *Pffft pow!* It blew up all over me. I had purple polka dots all over my face, my hair, my hands, and . . . "OH NO . . . MY WHITE SUIT!" I yelled.

I ran to the bathroom, stripped off the suit, and immediately soaked it in cold water in the bathtub to try to rescue it from permanent staining.

Do you know when you are looking forward to wearing a certain outfit, and then for some random reason like a smoothie blowout, you have to switch gears and find a new one in a hurry? Now that's conflict!!!! I found another outfit; wiped my face, hands, and hair; and raced out the door for my gig.

Returning home and expecting to find my suit all clean in the tub, I knelt in front of the bathtub, grabbed my blazer out of the water, and realized that the blueberry stains were still there. I was not going to let this happen to my favorite suit, so I added more mild detergent and began to agitate the water with my hands to enhance the cleaning process. I swished and swished and then swished in the opposite direction, agitating the water like a Maytag washing machine, swishing and wishing that the stains would let go.

Then it came to me. I started thinking about the act of agitation, and how—in relationships with ourselves and others—agitated feelings and conversations are uncomfortable. Yet, like doing laundry, we won't get the same clean result without the agitation.

The word *agitate* comes from the Latin derivative *agitare*, which means "to set into motion."

To become free and clean, like our laundry, we need a driving force to set ourselves into motion. We need issues of the past to be shaken up, rattled around, and detached from who we really are. We need agitation to set into motion the stuff we need to shake off, and we need it more often than many are willing to endure.

There's always some scrubbing required to achieve the squeakiest clean. Sounds simple enough, but it's not always so easy. Not everyone is willing to handle the discomfort of the agitation process. We need to be able to move past the discomfort and allow the cleansing process to rid us of the unclean, impure, or unnecessary.

Give yourself permission to be discomforted by agitation from time to time. Don't be afraid to agitate your situation to shake free and let go of anything that holds you back.

My suit finally did let go of the blueberry stains, and likewise I've allowed myself to be agitated, and even agitated a few people along the way so that they could shake off the residue and limiting beliefs that were ground in deep.

Be courageous and open to agitation. Don't be afraid to set things into motion, especially that stuff that you've buried for years. If you've put it to rest, but it keeps wreaking havoc on your feelings, your behaviors, and those around you, then you haven't dealt with it, and you haven't let it go, you've just pushed it down. Agitation will help you stir it up, and what's coming up in conversation with good intentions toward peace is coming out of you.

Trust that what's on the other side of the agitated state will be better than keeping the burdens with you. Besides never trusting a blueberry smoothie when you're wearing white, common sense also should tell us that relationships that are important are worth going through the uncomfortable conversations to find peace.

Agitation is the opposite of holding on. If you want to be free, you've got to let go of the things that are holding you back. Agitation is uncomfortable, but to set old stains into motion, we need to have a willingness to be uncomfortable. We avoid what's not comfortable. We don't set the important action into motion to get to the other side of conflict. Instead, we typically keep it inside, but it just agitates us internally, and as hard as we try to keep it down . . . to play human whack-a-mole with it, hammering it down as it constantly pops up . . . we only remain exhausted and frustrated, and it's still there.

To let go of conflict, we must stir it up, and to do that we have to be comfortable being uncomfortable. Embracing short-term discomfort in exchange for long-term comfort makes common sense, but isn't common practice. Society has a low tolerance for discomfort.

Numbing the Value of Discomfort

We're designed to grow through discomfort. Think of our first journey in life . . . being squeezed through the birth canal, through which we all came, unless born by cesarean, where we were still discomforted by the change in environment from a warm womb to a temperature change, with air and food supply cut from a severed umbilical cord. We entered discomfort the first seconds we were born to breathe air through our lungs and find new nourishment. Life continues to deliver similar labor. The very things that we want the most will require a passage through discomfort. We must stop treating discomfort as an enemy, avoiding it or fending it off, and keep on moving through the tight spots for a chance to be reborn into a new way of living.

Today we don't necessarily have to feel discomfort, because we live fairly comfortable lives, and can mask discomfort with substances like drugs or alcohol or luxury items, of which none bring us true peace. Minimizing discomfort by maximizing numbing substances is a short-term solution, with a long-lasting need for that temporary fix, but consumption is on the rise.

The COVID-19 crisis created an increase in drugs and alcohol consumption. Its impact on the workplace has sparked the substance use disorder (SUD) conversations in corporate North America.[3] According to a recent study by the Mental Health Index by Lifeworks in May 2021, alcohol consumption increased by 31 percent and drug use 29 percent, and close to one-third of Canadian and US respondents reported a consumption increase.[4]

You can't smell someone's breath over Zoom, and the proximity to a legalized cannabis market makes adding a buzz to the workday all too accessible for those working remotely. In Canada, the sale of cannabis went from illegal prior to October 2018 to becoming an essential service, available during the lockdown of March 2020,[5] from illegal to essential in the short time span of eighteen months. Only eight states deemed recreational cannabis essential during COVID-19 shutdowns, yet a 17 percent increase in sales over the previous year was noted, and the average purchase increased by 47 percent. US federal legalization is sought to provide economic stimulus through tax revenue and job creation during the COVID-19 recovery.[6]

Some individuals drink or use drugs to escape, avoid, or otherwise regulate unpleasant emotions such as those resulting from work and family conflict.[7]

Adversarial relationships with discomfort cause us to avoid feelings and conversations about uncomfortable things, conflict, and commitment. Trying to minimize discomfort will minimize the depth of our relationships. Having a healthy and courageous relationship with intolerance will help us embrace unpleasant situations and allow them to play out into more peace in a healthy way.

Embracing conflict is paramount to staying in it. Yes, it's uncomfortable to unpack your suitcase to make sure you're showing up to see your workplace through adult eyes, and to take the time to deal with issues as they arise, but if you think your comfort zone is staying in the conflict, think again, because conflict is the storm before the calm. By avoiding the blame game and taking an honest inventory of what's yours (gold) and what's not yours (silver), you can work through your own entanglements, which will enhance your capacity to deal with other people.

Enjoy the diverse buffet that people present to you and try the three-bite rule, possibly even twice for a concerted effort to make relationships work, but three bites isn't thirty bites. We need to be assertive and stand up to verbal abuse or end unhealthy relationships. Be adventurous and savor the flavor of your increased potential and remember the value in agitation. Stirring things up can set issues into motion and help you let them go, which is a long-term, natural way to stay high on life. I hope you found some HOLY SHIFT opportunities to record in your notes for action to "Challenge Conflict."

Life gets tastier with a dash of tolerance, a sprinkle of empathy, and a spoonful of forgiveness, which is the topic of our final strategy.

8

Empathize

Balance people's personal needs and business needs.

WHY ARE THERE ICEBERGS IN MY WORKPLACE SANDBOX?

Besides climate change and odd weather patterns, the new epidemic affecting work teams is below the surface. People in your workplace are fighting a tough battle, and like seeing the tip of an iceberg, we understand that under the surface, there is a huge part of them that you don't know. Being open to understand the deeper part of others requires empathy. Empathy is the ability to understand and share the feelings of another, but it's hard to empathize with the large part of someone that you don't even know or see.

Be kind, for everyone you meet is fighting a harder battle. —Plato

Put Yourself in Their Shoes

Sometimes the iceberg isn't a person, it's a problem, and by getting under the surface to examine and embrace the larger part of it, we can accept it and grow from it.

"Your position is eliminated, and we do not have another position for you." Sue's world changed when she heard the words. Sue had a high-profile position in her organization. As well as her busy role, she put many cohorts through an incredibly successful six-month leadership development program to develop high-potential employees. Sue found herself tossed into the sandstorm of austerity and competition, where people were afraid, and the sandbox was getting pretty mucky due to uncertainty of job cuts that were happening. Despite her dedication and extracurricular efforts to improve leadership within her organization, Sue was one of those who lost their position in a round of layoffs.

"I needed to take a time-out and step back. In that reflection period I realized that during the tumultuous time of the cutbacks, I hadn't taken care of myself. I should have been kinder to myself instead of trying to skate harder and faster. My initial instinct was to be negative, but I knew that I would never regret having integrity. Part of being true to myself was being kind, and respectful of myself and others. That's my WHY, part of my values of who I am and who I want to be," Sue said.

I asked her how she navigated through the storm. "I decided to empathize with those on the other side of that difficult decision, and I put myself in their shoes. I had to feel what it was like being on the other side of the issue, and what those folks were going through, which enabled me to maneuver through. I understand that challenging times happen to all of us and that they build our character and resilience if we let them."

It's hard to step on someone's feet when you're walking in their shoes.
—Mark Goulston

Leaders and followers need to switch roles often. A good leader knows how to step back and let others lead, and just be a good follower. The leadership development program helped Sue learn from, teach, and build other leaders. When she needed to take the high road herself through a difficult sandstorm, she had to lead by example and practice what she preached. We talked about different coping styles and different communication styles about learning from others around you. "Ironically," Sue said, "when I left my organization, I had recently had to lay off a high-caliber employee, whose program had been ended. Their acceptance and grace were incredible. They were amazingly generous with knowledge-sharing in handing off some of their work. This work could not have been successfully concluded without their help. When they later called me for a reference, I was delighted to share how powerful their influence was on me as I navigated my own departure. I followed their example; they were a role model for me."

Empathy, Compassion, and Sympathy

Empathy is defined as understanding and entering into another's feelings, where the appreciation of something depends on one's ability to project their personality into the viewed object.

For years we've led with our brains in the workplace, in business, or with office behavior with expectations rooted in stoicism, emotional discipline, and authority, but the grains of sand have shifted. With competition for the best jobs, and the best talent to fill them, leading with the heart creates a unique company culture that cultivates positive returns.[1] When a workplace has leaders (of all levels) who are compassionate, stronger relationships are formed, which creates a higher level of employee engagement, productivity, and retention. People who work in a compassionate culture show higher levels of job satisfaction and teamwork, commitment to their organization, accountability to their roles, and lower absenteeism rates,[2] but what really is compassion?

Compassion is an emotional response to empathy or sympathy, which creates a desire to help. Although compassion and empathy are fundamentally different, they are closely related.

Empathy is a feeling of awareness toward another's feelings; compassion creates a desire to help. It's the ability to see yourself in another person's shoes. Compassion adds another dimension of a desire to help.[3] I learned from a kindergarten example how compassion can be recognized.

Little Luke played diligently in the sandbox in his kindergarten class. Daily, his playful imagination built what looked like Jurassic Park for his favorite dinosaur toys, and he went about his own ideas to entertain himself. Luke always played alone because if another child came onto the scene and so much as touched or moved any of the toys or landscape, Luke would scream and cry. His teacher would try to convince him that other kids had good ideas to add, and that if he didn't let others into his sandbox, that he would never have friends or others to play with. One day Luke finally did let little Carly play. She grabbed a dinosaur and started to move it toward another, adding joyful dialogue about the dinosaurs going on a trip up the sand hill. Although Luke wanted to let her play, he tried to hold back his tears, but they overtook him and he began to weep, and then sob uncontrollably over the idea of sharing and relinquishing control. Carly put down her dinosaur, walked over to Luke, and gave him a big hug. Soon they were both sobbing, and the teacher came over to mediate. "Carly," the teacher said, "it's OK to play with Luke and the dinosaurs." "I know," Carly wailed, "I am just helping him cry."

Within that school year, Luke went from playing nice with one little girl to playing nice with three other kids in his sandbox. Teacher was very proud, and with little options for helping, Carly's compassion to help with a simple hug became Luke's turning point.

Empathy is not sympathy. Sympathy involves understanding from your own perspective. Empathy involves putting yourself in the other person's shoes and understanding WHY they may have these feelings.[4] Sympathy can be a very useful response of agreement or judgment, but because people often feed on it, it leaves them dependent. With empathy, you don't necessarily have to agree, but you fully and deeply understand them emotionally and intellectually.

Vulnerability

There is a vulnerability required when acting with empathy because we need to be willing to feel uncomfortable emotions that most people prefer to avoid. Vulnerability is closely tied to empathy because we need to be vulnerable to access our own experiences that allow us to be empathic, and to share personal moments that others can relate to.[5]

In my experience with conflict resolution, the vulnerability shared among team members with authentic and honest conversation always strengthens relationships. One's vulnerability can encourage another's empathy.

To be empathic is risky because there is a level of security needed to be open to the idea that you may be influenced. This is somewhat of a paradox, because to influence others, you must be willing to be influenced as well.

There are other paradoxes in becoming more empathic. To become more patient, you must be more patient with your impatience, and to become more tolerant, you must become more tolerant with your intolerance. To trust more, we must be willing to trust what we're not trusting. Moving deeper into these traits will help us develop the quality of relationship that we are seeking. Patience, tolerance, and trust don't just happen because a magic fairy makes everyone else easier to deal with. These qualities are developed with practice, through adversity, with self-reflection and sets the bar higher for how much deeper we need to dig to self-cultivate the result that we want with others.

Self-Empathy

The first step to empathizing with someone is to empathize with yourself.[6] Self-empathy is observing yourself in a nonjudgmental way, to see and know what is going on within you. It doesn't necessarily require a conversation about it while you are giving someone else their "psychological air," but it does help you discern what is yours and what is someone else's.

Honesty plays a foundational role in self-empathy. You must be willing to see and admit what you see in yourself—as cliché as it sounds, the truth will set you free. When observing yourself with empathy, you don't have to be perfect, or fit into the constructs of what others think is normal. The real you is enough. Real people feel. Crying is every bit as important as laughing, perhaps in different ratios, but real people feel. Real men cry. Real families and work teams have struggles and challenges, and it's OK, it's normal, and the self-empathy you have will help you play fair with **you**.

Intimacy Breaks Down Walls

In the need to be perfect in the eyes of people that we may not even know or like, we put on a façade, or we build emotional walls to protect ourselves. But the reality of walls is that not only are we making it difficult for people to get in . . . we ourselves cannot get out.

One of our own biggest obstacles is being seen through the walls that we ourselves build. The challenge with that is that we rarely share those deeper parts of ourselves with our colleagues.

Intimacy is not about sex or romance. Its Latin origin means "closely acquainted, very familiar." I like to describe it this way: *into-me-see*. It takes humility and vulnerability to have closely acquainted and very familiar relations with people. People are craving the real, emotional side of connection. You see it in the popularity of reality TV. People want to see into you. They want to feel you. They want the real, authentic deal . . . not the front that gets posted on "Fakebook." Intimacy, vulnerability, and authenticity are like an emotional elixir that becomes the juice that connects humans.

Now that we've understood some of the meanings of empathy and related emotions, let's find some ways to be more empathic.

It all starts by listening with the intention to really understand what someone is feeling. There are words, and there are feelings. To understand both, we need to tap into both sides of the brain. As learned in the earlier chapter about active listening, it's a learned skill to focus on understanding from another person's frame of reference. **Empathic listening** helps you to get further inside someone's perspective. It takes listening with your ears, eyes, and heart. You listen for meaning, and for feelings, which gives you very accurate data to work with because you are not projecting your own autobiographical thoughts, assumptions, motives, or interpretations. When you are empathically listening, you are giving the person talking "psychological air," which is an unsatisfied need they have. You can appease that need by providing the space and time required to get inside their world with your eyes, ears, and heart.

As an empathic listener, you're able to receive the deep communication of another human spirit. Next to physical survival, the greatest need of the human spirit is the need to feel understood, affirmed, validated, and appreciated. Once this need is satisfied, you are in a great spot to influence or solve problems. Symbolic to a thorough medical diagnosis before a prescription, you can't solve a set of problems that you don't understand.[7]

The time it takes to empathically listen to someone far outweighs the problems of creating misunderstandings or to have unexpressed or unresolved problems in your relationships. People are craving empathic leadership, where emotional stamina and professional maturity are among the skills that attract and build engagement.

A Solid Apology

Never underestimate the power of the word *sorry*, but don't overuse it. *Sorry* is a word that will build social grace. By some it's used far too infrequently; by others, it's overused. When you regret having said or done something and feel remorse, say sorry. For example, if you miss a deadline or deliver sloppy work, arrive late, completely forget something, or lose your cool, you can apologize. A good apology will go beyond the one word to include the specifics of what you are sorry for, and the people it may have impacted. You could also acknowledge how your actions affected them and explain what happened. Next, you'll want to share how you will rectify the situation or behave next time. "I'm sorry I missed the deadline yesterday for submission to your communications bulletin. I know how much pressure it puts on you when you can't get your tasks done without my material, and next time the due date lands during my inventory week, I will plan better."

According to career advice from Monster.com,[8] overapologizing could be seen as a weakness if something isn't your fault or you feel insecure or uncomfortable, aren't sure what else to say, or want to be liked by others. "I'm sorry to bother you, but . . . ," "Sorry the light is flickering," "Sorry I didn't know what else to say," or "Sorry that this might come off harsh, but . . ." In these cases, try to stop the habit of saying sorry and just state facts or ask for what you need. "May I have a moment of your time?" or "The lightbulb is flickering."

Grieving What's Been Lost

Allowing people to grieve is a way to show empathy. We were already grieving loss, guilt, uncertainty, denial, anger, regret, and more prior to 2020, but the pandemic has interrupted routines and amplified the grief.[9] Acknowledging what has been lost is a way to show empathy. Grief from one circumstance can recur with emotional triggers, including anniversaries and milestones. Allow people the space to grieve, and don't be shy to talk about death even though it might be awkward or bumpy. The effort will provide the biggest deposit into the relationship, not the words themselves.

Psychological Safety

Feeling safe needs to be paramount, and although it should start at the top of an organization, it's everyone's responsibility. A psychologically safe environment is a climate in which people are comfortable being and expressing themselves. If somebody makes a mistake, the goal is to have it discussed without fear, and to give a productive response to help correct the situation. "Thank you for letting me know. Do you need any help correcting the issue?"

Balance

We need to be super understanding of how people are attempting to balance their work and personal lives. A year and a half into the pandemic period, *Forbes* magazine identified that "the standard 9-to-5 workweek is now up for change. The pandemic-induced, remote-work, year-and-a-half experiment has proven to be an undisputed success."[10] The flexibility that the pandemic showed us is that we could work differently, some from home, some back to the office, and some hybrid. It also taught us how comfortable and convenient working from home can be, and for some it amplified the working hours required. People want flexibility in the nine-to-five workday, making it no longer the standard shift, and profits are up.

Leading with Empathy

Jacinda Ardern, prime minister of New Zealand since 2017, is the world's youngest female head of government. At the age of thirty-seven when she took office, she pledged empathy and delivered in spades. Known for being compassionate, her effectiveness is because her intentions are believed to be in the best interests of the public. People get a sense that "she's got your back." In an article written comparing pandemic responses of female leaders, Ardern is acknowledged as "remarkable at making people feel like she's standing with them, not talking down at them. It's critical when it comes to trust and where many leaders fail."[11] Ardern understands that compassion and strength go hand in hand. She says, "One of the criticisms I've faced over the years is that I'm not aggressive enough or assertive enough, or maybe somehow, because I'm empathetic, I'm weak. I totally rebel against that. I refuse to believe that you cannot be both compassionate and strong."[12]

Knowing that it's possible to have two feelings about the same thing like Jacinda is noteworthy. We don't have to pick one emotion or see things one way or another, and that helps us act with empathy because it suspends judgment and allows acceptance.

Choose the Next-Highest Thought

We don't always feel like doing the right thing or feel like taking the "high road" or feel like doing what's needed to rise up and out of sticky situations. A way to elevate your emotions and move higher up in thought is to consider the scale of emotions, find your current vibration, and choose the next-highest thought. Esther and Jerry Hicks teach the emotional guidance scale,[13] starting from the bottom with feelings of fear, grief, and depression, rising all the way through twenty-two different emotions to the highest: joy, empowerment, freedom, love, and acceptance. It's difficult to jump many steps on the scale at once, so just choosing the next-highest thought about a situation can help you begin the climb. If you are feeling anger, it may be challenging to feel optimism about the same situation, but if you could move from anger to disappointment, you're moving closer to joy. Some people are fantastic at choosing higher thoughts, especially those who have lived with adversity and learned how choices in their thinking were able to elevate their emotions. In her book *Ask and It Is Given,* Hicks provides the scale of emotions and many processes for getting unstuck and choosing something better for yourself.[14]

Forgiveness Fosters Acceptance

Remember my author friend Ron Price who was happy to collaborate on this book? Ron retells a story about a man who had a fifty-year career as an insurance agent, and over that fifty-year career, nobody could ever remember him getting crosswise with anybody. He never had a dispute with a customer client, a coworker, or anybody over a fifty-year term. When he retired, his coworkers celebrated with a big party and then a smaller, more intimate after-party. One of the newer agents asked, "What's your secret? How, *how* did you spend fifty years and never get upset with anybody?" He said, "Well, a long time ago when I was just starting out, I realized that everybody I dealt with every day was going to be human. They were going to be no more perfect than I am. They were going to have flaws and faults and shortcomings. They were going to do things that if I wasn't careful, could get on my nerves and get me all upset. So, I made a list of everyone's top ten faults, and then through the years, whenever they did one of those, I just reminded myself that they're not perfect either. I overlooked a lot of things and didn't worry about it." The young agent said, "Ooh, I like that." He said, "Just for fun, I'll write down what I think the boss's top ten faults are and compare with your list. Let's see how close we get." The retiree chuckled and said, "Well, to tell you the truth, I never really wrote them down, but every time he did something that bothered me, I would've said, 'Boy, lucky for him, that's one of the ten.'"

Can we just allow people to be human and imperfect, without judgment or anger or hatred or grudges? Everyone's fighting a tough battle somehow, somewhere, or sometime in their life.

Practicing gratitude for any length of time offers a quick gateway to happiness because we are focusing on what we have rather than what we don't have. Like the list of ten things to forgive someone for, try a quick list of ten things you are grateful for to read daily.[15]

Empathy takes knowing yourself, and taking action for others that say, "I heard you, I'm working to understand what you said, and I'm doing my best to respond thoughtfully." The more you know yourself, the better you will be able to be emotionally available for someone else. This relates back to the first sandbox strategy, Position Yourself for Success, and brings these strategies full circle. Doing and saying the right thing is also symbolic to the tip of an iceberg, because behavior stems from the massive base of character traits we have underneath or within. It takes vulnerability to be empathic for someone and to hear them with your ears, eyes, and heart.

Getting alongside people to talk with them and seeking to understand them and to feel their feelings, especially those who are different than you, will create strong bonds that can endure the test of time. Everyone fights a hard battle from time to time, and by creating psychological safety we allow people to be comfortable expressing themselves. When errors are made, you will always have your apology tool, and your forgiveness power to allow people to be perfectly imperfect.

If you're just not feeling up to being awesome, try choosing the next-highest thought, or doing a quick gratitude tune-up. Playing nice is a work in progress, and you'll be building a castle that you love, one that welcomes others to build with you.

What will you do differently to be better with empathy toward yourself and others? Write it down to complete your eight (or more) action items on the HOLY SHIFTS download, provided as a companion for this book, and practice Empathy.

CONCLUSION

Keeping These Eight Strategies Top of Mind

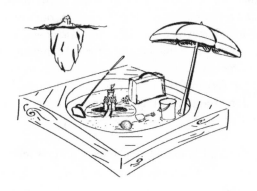

ARE YOU READY TO DIG IN?

There are many reasons why conflict surfaces in every workplace, much of which is avoidable. The high cost of conflict can be reduced, reserving profits for better use, and it's everyone's responsibility to make relationships work.

Implementing these eight strategies will help you become the responsible, influential, and productive problem solver who can embrace and even welcome conflict with your coworkers, bosses, clients, and others, knowing that healthy relationships grow from conflict. By practicing these eight play nice strategies, you will exponentially increase your capacity to thrive in this new virtual, global sandbox. As we embark on rebuilding our postpandemic economy, the strategies and tools to excavate, cultivate, elevate, and duplicate one's greatest castle are more important than ever.

#1 Position yourself for success. Good play starts within.

Turn inward to do your own internal work so you can come out big on the outside. Positioning ourselves as authentic, confident, and influential people will follow our internal disposition. You are like the sand. Tilling and turning over your thoughts is the groundwork for the fertility of what you want to create. It's the inside work that never ends, and it's foundational to build your own greatest castle. We must be greater than our current circumstances and environment. When our intentions and actions are equal to our thoughts, our minds and bodies are working together, which provides immense power behind us. In a sandstorm, don't jump to the point of a formal complaint or investigation. Use your tools. Cultivate what you want to grow and invite people to talk about it. Ask for help when needed, apologize when you know you haven't done the right thing, and be patient with yourself. Build your own castle first.

#2 Lighten your load. Unpack to make space for new relationship tools.

Keep working toward lightening your load to unpack the old stories from early patterning and make room for the tools to cultivate what you'd rather develop. The only way through conflict is through it. You can't go over it, under it, or around it. You can only reach the other side by confronting the issues in front of you. Any issue that seems difficult to address should be addressed face-to-face, by video chat, or at least by phone conversation, leaving less chance for misinterpretation and more chance for compassion, empathy, and human connection. Texting and digital communication are missing the juice of human interaction and create keyboard warriors lacking the bravery to converse as they hide behind a screen to type what's on their mind. "Can we talk?" is an easy conversation starter that will help bridge relationships and give all parties a chance to be heard and understood. Life isn't just about feeling good all the time. It's about doing what's right. Short-term discomfort toward something worth having is well worth the effort.

#3 Actively listen. Help others feel understood.

By actively listening with the intention of helping others feel understood, we sift through their words and hone our greatest communication skill of all, which is giving others "psychological air" to share words and feelings. By offering validation rather than advice or analyzing, you'll help people find solutions to their problems and let go of their difficult emotions. Active listening increases the chance that they may listen to you, but that's not a guarantee. Releasing expectations of other people's behavior will return less disappointment. Even if resolutions aren't made, respectful communication and understanding another's viewpoints is valuable because people will know that you care about them and, if nothing else, can separate disagreements from the importance of the relationship. Just because we don't agree doesn't mean we no longer like each other.

#4 Yield to your WHY. Ground yourself in purpose.

Get clear on your WHY power to stay grounded through the harsh sandstorms. Often your greatest answers are found in the clarity of your WHY. Tap into the strong grounding of purpose to guide you through the tough times, via your inner brain that gives this innate desire a voice. Saying no, letting go, setting boundaries, and teaching people how to treat you requires more than willpower. When you ground yourself in purpose, and find your WHY, you will be able to deal with any "what."

#5 Nurture relationships. People who feel valued perform well.

When we respect the dignity of other human beings, we are respecting our own dignity in the process; therefore, the more respect we give out, the more we receive in the long run. To combat the worker shortage crisis that burdens all of us, we can use respect and recognition to help those around us feel accepted and valued as part of the whole. Remember that respect, recognition, receiving, and remote all have the prefix *re*, which means to "return to." By returning to these principles, you'll be making deposits into the relationship accounts of others. Providing feedback helps us build better castles together, and when the need for a challenging conversation arises, you can pull out your five-step tool to prepare and then go for it!

#6 Include everyone.

Inclusion is like the clay that will help form permanence in your sandbox; ordinary sand needs that extra element of clay to be extraordinary. The solution to relationship challenges includes those they affect. Including the right people into healing conversations, maintaining the organizational hierarchy, and speaking of others as if they were in the room are all healthy ways to embrace the challenges that plague workplaces. Fairness goes a long way, and our unconscious bias needs to be examined so that decisions and actions can be more equitable. Diversity is the spice of collaboration. We may look different on the surface, but underneath the surface, we are all the same. By weaving inclusivity into our daily efforts, we will create the culture of candor that can prevent or mitigate conflict and the associated cost to the people and companies we represent. When people feel in on things, they engage and stay more committed to change than when they feel excluded.

#7 Challenge conflict. Healthy teams learn to embrace it.

Resolve conflict as soon as possible, because there's more stress in not dealing with it than there is once you start the process. The only thing worse than being in conflict for two months, two weeks, or two days is one more day. Knowing what's yours in the knot of human entanglement is a vulnerable way to focus on the things you can control and change. If someone pushes your buttons, you have a button to push, and rather than expecting someone to shift their behavior to accommodate you, or blaming them for your frustration, you can take responsibility to improve yourself. With three bites to make relationships work, we extend the olive branch when relationships are rocky, but we also need to discern when to end an unhealthy relationship. Through conflict we become stronger and more confident. When we let go, we grow—even though it doesn't always feel positive or good, what's on the other side is worth the effort. Agitation, although uncomfortable, sets things into motion, where trying to minimize discomfort will also minimize the depth of our relationships.

#8 Empathize. Balance people's personal needs and business needs. Below the surface, everyone is fighting a hard battle. Hold a gentle space for each other to be human, to be imperfect. Empathy takes knowing yourself and taking action for others that says, "I heard you, I'm working to understand what you said, and I'm doing my best to respond thoughtfully." The more you know yourself, the better you'll be able to be emotionally available for someone else, which brings these eight strategies full circle, because your disposition on the surface comes from the inner work that you do. If you're not feeling up to being awesome, try choosing the next-highest thought, doing a quick gratitude tune-up, or look upward because you are never alone, and guidance from your higher power will aways be there for you.

This Playful Approach Is Simple, but Not Easy

Some may consider all the PLAY NICE strategies contained in this book as "soft skills," but nothing could be further from the truth. *Soft skills* is a term that is no longer appreciated. *Soft* would suggest easily acquired or demanding little effort, but as most people and organizations have discovered, the acquisition and implementation of these skills are very challenging and require practice. The word *skill* would imply that one could acquire it through training; however, traits encompassed by the term *soft skills* include character and personality traits, interpersonal skills, interdependence skills, emotional and social intelligence, motivational and leadership traits, and communication skills. It's no wonder to me why most senior leaders have gray hair because it takes decades to develop the professional maturity to master all the skills that I call one's "sandbox factor." Other terms that are widely acceptable are:

- People skills
- Emotional intelligence (EQ)
- Leadership traits
- Human skills

I always say that communication is an art, not a science, and it will never be perfect, but as perfect is used as a verb, we could certainly perfekt our sandbox skills with daily use.

A lot of this material is common sense, but common sense isn't always common practice. You'll realize that by the HOLY SHIFTS you've recognized as items to continue practicing. We must make common sense, common practice.

High-potential employees can get through the sandstorms to play nice when they're vulnerable enough to admit when they need help. Today's economy is competitive, and those with good sandbox skills will be like the cream that rises to the top. When two equally qualified people are competing for a promotion, their "sandbox factor" will be the deciding factor. When an employee can fall to sleep at night, content with their approach and movement through conflict, they will rest peacefully.

I've often questioned who is responsible for personal development, mental health, and wellness at work. I believe it's each team member's responsibility to make sure that they are well enough to do what they signed up to do—the way their résumé boastfully sold them to the employer. Although it's the employer's responsibility to provide a safe and healthy environment to work in, it's the employee's responsibility for their own personal leadership. With books, seminars, reflection, journaling, and working with mentors, coaches, or therapists, you'll be positioning yourself for your absolute best. Potential grows exponentially when you invest in yourself because others will invest more in you.

At the beginning of this book, I talked about the irony of me writing it, given the conflicts in my own life. Conflict resolution is a journey well worth taking. Just because we know better, doesn't mean we always do better. Communication is an art, not a science, and it will never be perfect because we're human, but with good intentions and practice, anything is possible. We need people. Relationships are important. With these tools, everyone can play at building productive, peaceful, and profitable relationships in the workplace sandbox. Dig in!

NOTES

Preface

1. Penny Tremblay, "The State of Workplace Conflict during COVID-19," Play Nice in the Sandbox, July 15, 2021, https://pennytremblay.com/2021/07/15/the-state-of-workplace-conflict-during-covid-19/.

2. Tremblay, "State of Workplace Conflict."

3. Jennifer Moss, *The Burnout Epidemic: The Rise of Chronic Stress and How We Can Fix It* (Boston: Harvard Business Review, 2021), 2.

4. Bill Howatt, Louise Bradley, Jesse Adams, Sapna Mahajan, and Samuel Kennedy, *Understanding Mental Health, Mental Illness, and Their Impacts in the Workplace* (Ottawa, ON: Mental Health Commission of Canada, 2017), https://www.mentalhealthcommission.ca/wp-content/uploads/drupal/2018-06/Monreau_White_Paper_Report_Eng.pdf.

5. Donald Sull, Charles Sull, and Ben Zweig, "Toxic Culture Is Driving the Great Resignation," *MIT Sloan Management Review*, January 11, 2022, https://sloanreview.mit.edu/article/toxic-culture-is-driving-the-great-resignation.

6. Marcel Schwantes, "Why Do Employees Quit on Their Bosses?," *Inc.*, December 21, 2018, https://www.inc.com/marcel-schwantes/why-do-people-quit-their-jobs-exactly-new-research-points-finger-at-5-common-reasons.html.

7. Jack Kelly, "People Don't Leave Bad Jobs, They Leave Bad Bosses: Here's How To Be a Better Manager to Maintain and Motivate Your Team," *Forbes*, November 22, 2019, https://www.forbes.com/sites/jackkelly/2019/11/22/people-dont-leave-bad-jobs-they-leave-bad-bosses-heres-how-to-be-a-better-manager-to-maintain-and-motivate-your-team/?sh=489de26622b9.

8. Cited in Deji Olanrewaju, "Conflict Management in the Workplace: Contemporary Approach," accessed August 21, 2022, https://www.academia.edu/15966203/conflict_management_in_the_workplace_contemporary_approach.

9. Jenny Lamothe, "Lifestory: Honouring Local Elder Shiikenh 'Gordon' Waindubence, Whose Social and Cultural Impact Cannot Be Overstated," Sudbury.com, December 23, 2021, https://www.sudbury.com/local-news/life story-honouring-local-elder-shiikenh-gordon-waindubence-whose-social -and-cultural-impact-cannot-be-understated-4895505.

Chapter 1

1. Daniel Amen, foreword to *Breaking the Habit of Being Yourself*, by Joe Dispenza (Carlsbad, CA: Hay House, 2012), xii–xiii.

2. Joe Dispenza, *Breaking the Habit of Being Yourself* (Carlsbad, CA: Hay House, 2012), 5–15.

3. Dispenza, *Breaking the Habit*, 47–48.

4. Lauren Smith, "New Recruiting Strategies for a Post-Covid World (Back to Work, Better)," *Harvard Business Review*, podcast episode, March 9, 2021, https://hbr.org/podcast/2021/03/new-recruiting-strategies-for-a-post-covid-world.

5. Smith, "New Recruiting Strategies."

6. Jennifer Moss, *The Burnout Epidemic: The Rise of Chronic Stress and How We Can Fix It* (Boston: Harvard Business Review Press, 2021), 167–72.

7. Charles Duhigg, "What Google Learned from Its Quest to Build the Perfect Team," *New York Times*, February 25, 2016.

8. Jacalyn Beales, "What Is Career Agility and How Can You Hire for It?" Lever, May 26, 2022, https://www.lever.co/blog/what-is-career-agility.

9. Willis Towers Watson Webcast, *Deeper Dive into the Employee Experience Implications of COVID-19*, April 22, 2020, https://www.wtwco.com/assets /covid-19/NA-COVID-19-ClientWebcast-April-22-Final.pdf.

10. "9 Team Working Skills That Improve Your Performance," Workplace from Meta, accessed August 23, 2022, https://www.workplace.com/blog /team-working-skills.

11. Wikipedia, s.v. "Know thyself," modified March 16, 2011, https:// en.wikipedia.org/wiki/Know_thyself.

Chapter 2

1. Joe Dispenza, *Breaking the Habit of Being Yourself* (Carlsbad, CA: Hay House, 2012), 41.

2. Olivia Guy-Evans, "What Happens at The Synapse? How Neurons Communicate with Each Other," Simply Psychology, February 21, 2021, https://www.simplypsychology.org/synapse.html.

3. Dispenza, *Breaking the Habit*, 42, 43.

4. D. O. Hebb, *The Organization of Behavior: A Neuropsychological Theory* (Mahwah, NJ: Lawrence Erlbaum, 2002).

5. Nicole R. Nugent, Amy Goldberg, and Monica Uddin, "Topical Review: The Emerging Field of Epigenetics: Informing Models of Pediatric Trauma and Physical Health," *Journal of Pediatric Psychology* 41, no. 1 (January/February 2016): 55–64, https://doi.org/10.1093/jpepsy/jsv018.

6. L. Z. Song, G. E. Schwartz, and L. G. Russek, "Heart-Focused Attention and Heart-Brain Synchronization: Energetic and Physiological Mechanisms," *Alternative Therapies in Health and Medicine* 4, no. 5 (September 1998): 44–52, 54–60, 62, PMID: 9737031.

7. Joe Dispenza, *Becoming Supernatural* (Carlsbad, CA: Hay House, 2017), 27–42.

8. Ruth Lindquist, Mariah Snyder, and Mary Fran Tracy, eds., *Complementary & Alternative Therapies in Nursing*, 7th ed. (New York: Springer, 2014), 232, http://www.stikespanritahusada.ac.id/wp-content/uploads/2017/04/Ruth-Lindquist-PhD-RN-APRN-BC-FAAN_-Mariah-Snyder-PhD_-Mary-Frances-Tracy-PhD-RN-CCNS-FAAN-Complementary-Alternative-Therapies-in-Nursing_-Seventh-Edition-Springer-Publishing-Company-2013.pdf.

9. Patricia Ann Sealy, "Autoethnography: Reflective Journaling and Meditation to Cope with Life-Threatening Breast Cancer," *Clinical Journal of Oncology Nursing* 16, no. 1 (2012): 38–41.

10. Mark Stone, "Journaling with Clients," *Individual Psychology* 54, no. 4 (1998): 535, https://www.proquest.com/openview/77b0e49ae5828e956d7b1c5beb5a0baf/1?pq-origsite=gscholar&cbl=1816606.

11. Dispenza, *Breaking the Habit*, chap. 6.

12. https://drjoedispenza.com/collections/books.

13. Jennifer Moss, *The Burnout Epidemic: The Rise of Chronic Stress and How We Can Fix It* (Boston: Harvard Business Review, 2021), 125–40.

14. "The Seven Grandfather Teachings," American Indian Health Service of Chicago, accessed August 22, 2022, https://aihschgo.org/seven-grandfather-teachings/.

15. "Humility (Wolf)," Manitoba Trauma Information and Education Centre, accessed 2022, https://trauma-informed.ca/humility-wolf/.

16. Chia-Yen (Chad) Chiu, Prasad Balkundi, Bradley P. Owens, and Paul E. Tesluk, "Shaping Positive and Negative Ties to Improve Team Effectiveness: The Roles of Leader Humility and Team Helping Norms," *Human Relations* 75, no. 3 (March 2022): 502–31. https://doi.org/10.1177/0018726720968135.

Chapter 3

1. Roger Fisher, William Ury, and Bruce Patton, *Getting to Yes*, 2nd ed. (New York: Penguin, 2006).

2. Michael S. Sorensen, *I Hear You: The Surprisingly Simple Skill behind Extraordinary Relationships* (N.p.: Autumn Creek Press, 2017).

3. Brittany Carrico, "What Is Emotional Invalidation?," Psych Central, updated July 18, 2021, https://psychcentral.com/health/reasons-you-and-others -invalidate-your-emotional-experience#recap.

4. Fisher, Ury, and Patton, *Getting to Yes*.

5. Roger Fisher and William Ury, *Getting Past No* (London: Random House Business Books, 1992).

6. Jack Zenger and Joseph Folkman, "What Great Listeners Actually Do," *Harvard Business Review*, July 14, 2016. https://hbr.org/2016/07/what -great-listeners-actually-do.

7. "Statistics on Remote Workers That Will Surprise You," Apollo Technical, May 11, 2022, https://www.apollotechnical.com/statistics-on-remote-workers/.

Chapter 4

1. *Encyclopedia Britannica*, s.v. "golden ratio," accessed August 3, 2022, https://www.britannica.com/science/golden-ratio.

2. Kate Capato, "Truth, Beauty, and Math . . . ," *Visual Grace* (blog), October 15, 2021, https://www.visualgrace.org/truth-beauty-and-math/.

3. Simon Sinek, *Start with Why* (New York: Portfolio, 2010).

4. Sinek, *Start with Why*, 41.

5. Sinek, *Start with Why*.

6. "OH&S Legislation in Canada—Introduction," OSH Answers Fact Sheets, Canadian Centre for Occupational Health and Safety, accessed August 22, 2022, https://www.ccohs.ca/oshanswers/legisl/intro.html.

7. "Civil Rights Center," U.S. Department of Labor, accessed August 22, 2022, https://www.dol.gov/agencies/oasam/centers-offices/civil-rights-center.

8. "Workplace Violence and Workplace Harassment," Ontario Ministry of Labour, Immigration, Training and Skills Development, https://www.ontario

.ca/document/guide-occupational-health-and-safety-act/part-iii0i-workplace
-violence-and-workplace-harassment.

9. "Is It Harassment? A Tool to Guide Employees," Government of Canada, Treasury Board Secretariat, accessed December 31, 2021, https://www.canada .ca/en/government/publicservice/wellness-inclusion-diversity-public-service /harassment-violence/harassment-tool-employees.html.

10. Wikipedia, s.v. "Lateral Violence," modified October 1, 2018, https:// en.wikipedia.org/wiki/Lateral_violence.

11. "Bullying in the Workplace," OSH Answers Fact Sheets, Canadian Centre for Occupational Health and Safety, accessed August 22, 2022, https:// www.ccohs.ca/oshanswers/psychosocial/bullying.html.

Chapter 5

1. Jennifer Moss, *The Burnout Epidemic: The Rise of Chronic Stress and How We Can Fix It* (Boston: Harvard Business Review Press, 2021).

2. https://steviesiebold.net/.

3. "The Great Resignation: Why Workers Say They Quit Jobs in 2021," Pew Research Center, March 9, 2022, https://www.pewresearch.org/fact-tank /2022/03/09/majority-of-workers-who-quit-a-job-in-2021-cite-low-pay-no -opportunities-for-advancement-feeling-disrespected/.

4. Kristie Rogers and Beth Schinoff, "Disrespected Employees Are Quitting. What Can Managers Do Differently?" *MIT Sloan Management Review*, July 28, 2022, https://sloanreview.mit.edu/article/disrespected-em ployees-are-quitting-what-can-managers-do-differently/?utm_source=newslet ter&utm_medium=email&utm_content=Read%20the%20new%20article%20 now%20%C2%BB&utm_campaign=Enews%20Leadership%208/3/22%20 Control.

5. https://greatnessmagnified.com/.

6. Joint Commission on Accreditation of Healthcare Organizations, 2005 National Patient Safety Goals.

Chapter 6

1. "Unconscious Bias Training," Office of Diversity and Outreach, University of California, San Francisco, accessed August 6, 2022, https://diver sity.ucsf.edu/programs-resources/training/unconscious-bias-training.

2. "Take a Test," Project Implicit, accessed August 16, 2022, https://im plicit.harvard.edu/implicit/takeatest.html.

3. Lily Zheng, "What to Do with Your Implicit Bias," Quartz at Work, August 6, 2018, accessed August 16, 2022, https://qz.com/work/1349271/what-to-do-with-your-implicit-bias/.

4. Robin J. Ely and Irene Padavic, "What's Really Holding Women Back?," *Harvard Business Review*, March 1, 2020, https://hbr.org/2020/03/whats-really-holding-women-back.

5. Liane Davey, "How to Tell the Difference between Venting and Office Gossip," *Harvard Business Review*, November 29, 2016, https://hbr.org/2016/11/how-to-tell-the-difference-between-venting-and-office-gossip?registration=success.

6. Davey, "How to Tell the Difference."

7. Penny Tremblay, *Give and Be Rich: Tapping the Circle of Abundance* (New York: Morgan James, 2014).

8. Ed Catmull, and Amy Wallace, *Creativity, Inc.* (New York: Random House, 2014).

9. "The Future Workforce: More Diverse Than Ever," AAUW: Empowering Women Since 1881, March 27, 2020, https://www.aauw.org/resources/article/future-workforce-diverse/.

10. William H. Frey, "The US Will Become 'Minority White' in 2045, Census Projects," *The Avenue* (blog), Brookings Institution, March 14, 2018, https://www.brookings.edu/blog/the-avenue/2018/03/14/the-us-will-become-minority-white-in-2045-census-projects/.

11. Heather Long and Andrew Van Dam, "Women of Color Are Surging into the U.S. Workforce, Causing a Historic First in Who's Getting Hired," *Washington Post*, September 9, 2019, https://www.washingtonpost.com/business/economy/for-the-first-time-ever-most-new-working-age-hires-in-the-us-are-people-of-color/2019/09/09/8edc48a2-bd10-11e9-b873-63ace636af08_story.html.

12. Sandra L. Colby and Jennifer M. Ortman, *Projections of the Size and Composition of the U.S. Population: 2014 to 2060*, U.S. Census Bureau, March 2015, accessed August 4, 2022, https://www.census.gov/content/dam/Census/library/publications/2015/demo/p25-1143.pdf.

13. "Future Workforce."

14. "LGBT Data & Demographics," Williams Institute, UCLA School of Law, accessed August 4, 2022, https://williamsinstitute.law.ucla.edu/visualization/lgbt-stats/?topic=LGBT#density.

15. Aubrey Blanche, "DEI in 2022: Key Trends and Findings," Culture Amp, accessed August 4, 2022, https://www.cultureamp.com/blog/dei-2022-trends.

16. Kate Heinz, "What Does Diversity, Equity and Inclusion (DEI) Mean in the Workplace?," Built In, accessed August 4, 2022, https://builtin.com/diversity-inclusion/what-does-dei-mean-in-the-workplace.

17. "Diversity, Equity, and Inclusion: A Professional Development Offering of the eXtension Foundation Impact Collaborative," dei.extension.org, accessed August 4, 2022, https://dei.extension.org.

Chapter 7

1. Patricia Evans, *The Verbally Abusive Relationship* (New York: Adams Media, 2002).

2. CrisMarie Campbell and Susan Clarke, *The Beauty of Conflict: Harnessing Your Team's Competitive Advantage* (Whitefish, MT: Two Hummingbird, 2017).

3. Theresa Agovino, "The COVID-19 Crisis Has Brought Substance Abuse to Light," Society for Human Resource Management, October 2, 2021, https://www.shrm.org/hr-today/news/all-things-work/pages/covid-19-brought-substance-abuse-to-light.aspx.

4. *The Mental Health Index Report: May 2021*, LifeWorks, June 24, 2021, accessed August 16, 2022, https://lifeworks.com/en/resource/mental-health-index%E2%84%A2-report-may-2021.

5. *Cannabis Retail during COVID-19*, Policy Brief, Canadian Centre on Substance Use and Addiction, January 2021, accessed August 17, 2022, https://www.ccsa.ca/sites/default/files/2021-01/CCSA-COVID-19-Cannabis-Retail-Policy-Brief-2021-en.pdf.

6. Frank Holland, "How the COVID-19 Crisis May Impact Cannabis Legalization," CNBC, April 19, 2020, https://www.cnbc.com/2020/04/19/how-the-covid-19-crisis-may-impact-cannabis-legalization.html.

7. Jennifer M. Wolff, Kathleen M. Rospenda, Judith A. Richman, Li Liu, and Lauren A. Milner, "Work-Family Conflict and Alcohol Use: Examination of a Moderated Mediation Model," *Journal of Addictive Diseases* 32, no. 1 (2013): 85–98, accessed August 17, 2022, https://www.ncbi.nlm.nih.gov/pmc/articles/PMC3602920/.

Chapter 8

1. Scholley Bubenik, "The Compassionate Leader Who Leads with The Heart—Is It Good for Business?" *Forbes*, February 13, 2019, https://www.forbes.com/sites/scholleybubenik/2019/02/13/the-compassionate-leader-who-leads-with-the-heart-is-it-good-for-business/?sh=1790aff0e504.

2. Sigal Barsade and Olivia O'Neill, "What's Love Got to Do with It? A Longitudinal Study of the Culture of Companionate Love and Employee and

Client Outcomes," *Administrative Science Quarterly* 59, no. 4 (2014), https://journals.sagepub.com/doi/abs/10.1177/0001839214538636.

3. Jacinta Jimenez, "Compassion vs. Empathy: Understanding the Difference," BetterUp, July 16, 2021, https://www.betterup.com/blog/compassion-vs-empathy.

4. Jenna Kisling, "The Difference between Empathy and Sympathy," Psychiatric Medical Care, accessed August 18, 2022, https://www.psychmc.com/articles/empathy-vs-sympathy.

5. "The Heart of Connection and Trust," Search Inside Yourself Leadership Institute, January 17, 2016, https://siyli.org/vulnerability-leadership/.

6. Godfrey T. Barrett-Lennard, "The Recovery of Empathy—Toward Others and Self," in *Empathy Reconsidered: New Directions in Psychotherapy*, edited by Arthur C. Bohart and Leslie S. Greenberg (Washington, DC: American Psychological Association, 1997), 103–21, https://doi.org/10.1037/10226-004.

7. Stephen R. Covey, *The 7 Habits of Highly Effective People* (New York: Simon & Schuster, 2013).

8. Elana Lyn Gross, "How to Stop Apologizing at Work: Sorry, but You Should Definitely Stop Saying Sorry All the Time—Especially If You Want to Get Ahead at Your Job," Monster, accessed August 19, 2022, https://www.monster.com/career-advice/article/stop-apologizing-at-work-0418.

9. Jennifer Moss, "Making Your Workplace Safe for Grief," *Harvard Business Review*, June 6, 2017, accessed August 19, 2022, https://hbr.org/2017/06/making-your-workplace-safe-for-grief.

10. Jack Kelly, "Working 9-to-5 Is an Antiquated Relic from the Past and Should Be Stopped Right Now," *Forbes*, July 25, 2021, https://www.forbes.com/sites/jackkelly/2021/07/25/working-9-to-5-is-an-antiquated-relic-from-the-past-and-should-be-stopped-right-now/?sh=315b700940de.

11. Rachel Botsman, "Why Compassion and Strength Go Hand-in-Hand," Medium, May 19, 2020, https://medium.com/@rachelbotsman/why-compassion-and-strength-go-hand-in-hand-272fa6b29b0f.

12. Botsman, "Compassion and Strength."

13. Esther Hicks and Jerry Hicks, *Ask and It Is Given* (Carlsbad, CA: Hay House, 2011), 113–23.

14. Hicks and Hicks, *Ask and It Is Given*.

15. Penny Tremblay, *Give and Be Rich: Tapping the Circle of Abundance* (New York: Morgan James, 2014).

INDEX

A

ability/(dis)ability, 99
absenteeism rates, lower, 121
abuse, 110–11, 117
abusive situation, 111
acceptance, 36, 94, 121, 127–28
    of impermanence, xviii
accountability, 53, 91, 121
acknowledging, 45, 50, 74, 126
acknowledgment statements, 44
active listening, xvi, 40–41, 43–44, 50,
    53, 124, 133
advising, 44
ages, 3, 6, 22, 94, 99, 108
aggravation, 113
aggression, hidden, 110
agility, 13–14
agitation, 30, 113–15, 117, 134
agreements, 41, 45–47, 122
air, psychological, 123–24, 133
Amen, Daniel, 3
analyzing, xxv, 32, 43–44, 53, 133
anger, 31, 62, 89, 126–28
Anishinaabe tradition, 34
anxiety, high, xiv
apologize, 15, 16, 18, 50, 125, 132
assertive play, 78
assumptions, 8, 52, 88, 91, 96, 98
attachment, 23–24, 26, 30, 36

attrition, xxv
awareness, 26–27, 35, 40, 105–6, 111,
    121

B

background noise, 43
baggage
    emotional, xii, 26
    old, 19, 21, 23, 30–31
balance, xvii, 34, 92, 119, 126, 135
    work-life, 94
barriers to listening, 43–44
behavior
    document, 62
    unethical, xxv
beliefs, unconscious, 87
bias, unconscious, 87, 134
blame, xv, xvii, 10–11, 15–16, 26, 104,
    106
body language, 1, 41
boredom, 31
boundaries, xiv, 56, 61, 65–67, 111,
    133
brain, 22, 27, 29, 32, 60, 121, 124
    habits, 3
brainwashing, 110
bravery, 34, 132
building trust, 45
bullies, xix, 62, 102–3

bullying, 63, 65, 76
burnout, xv, xxii, xxiv, 70
business relationships, 65, 107

C
Campbell, CrisMarie, 112
Canadian Centre for Occupational
    Health and Safety, 62
candor, 98, 100, 134
Canfield, Jack, 97
career advancement, xvi
caring, xviii, 70, 102
Catmull, Ed, 98
challenges, xiii, xv, xvii, xxi, 11–12,
    83, 104
  intergenerational workplace, 94
challenging conversations, 56, 63, 70,
    78, 80–81, 83–84
change, xv
circle, xxvii, 57–58, 60, 64, 94–95,
    129, 135
  golden, 60
  workplace restoration, 36
circle approach, 94
Civil Rights Center, 62
Clarke, Susan, 112
cohesion, 85, 100
collaboration, xviii, xxvi, 17, 81,
    95–97, 111
collaborative relationships, xvi
comfort, long-term, 115
comfort zone, 28, 56, 84, 116
commitments, religious, 99
communication, xxii–xxiii, 42, 44,
    46–47, 52–54, 81–82, 88, 136
  decreased, xv
  digital, xxv, 34, 132
  skills, 135
  styles, xiii, xxiii, 121
communicators, effective, 42

company culture, xxv
compassion, 7, 15, 34, 121, 132
competition, xix, xxiii, 97, 120–21
    fair, 88
compliment, 73–75, 78
conflict
  common workplace, xv
  resolving old, 25
  stress-related, xiv
  unresolved, xi, xix, 21, 23
conflict lessons, xvi
conflict of difficult conversations,
    27
conflict resolution, xiii, xvi–xvii, xx–
    xxi, 2, 86, 89
  permanent, xi
connection
  human, 34, 132
  synaptic, 22
contact, eye, 42
conversations, xii–xiii, 5–7, 14, 33,
    35–37, 42–44, 46–47, 49–53,
    77–84, 88–93
  authentic, xiii, 94
  uncomfortable, 78, 115
conversation starter, 96, 132
cost of conflict, xiii, xv, xxvi, 131
counselors, 33, 106
courage, 24, 34, 36–37, 81, 113
COVID-19, xiv–xv, xxii–xxiii, xxv,
    52, 116
coworkers, xvi, xxii, 90, 103, 128,
    131
crisis, xvii
cultivate, 9, 12–13, 18, 121, 123,
    131–32
culture
  compassionate, 121
  winning, xvi, xx
curiosity, 13–14, 29, 55, 95

D

defensiveness, provokes, 50
demands, personal, xxii
demean, 62
depression, 31, 62, 127
despair, 31
difficult conversations, 27–28, 30, 34, 37, 41, 77, 80
difficult situations, xix, 46, 56
disagreements, 14, 45, 47, 53–54, 133
disappointment, 31, 127, 133
discomfort, short-term, 37, 115, 132
disconnected relationships, xix
disconnected teams, 93
disconnection, social, xxii
discouragement, 31
dstractions, 43
    external, 43
diversity, xxv, 13, 109, 134
    equity, and inclusion (DEI), 86, 99
dominance, 62, 65
doubt, 31, 61, 79, 82, 92, 109

E

effective validation, 45
ego protection, 30
Einstein, Albert, 10
embarrass, 5, 33, 62
embrace conflict, xvi, xxi, xxvi, 34, 111–13
emotional
    addictions, 29–30, 36
    and social intelligence, 135
    freedom technique (EFT), 4, 6
    intelligence, 15, 135
    programming, 24, 27
        early, 26
    response, 121

emotions, 4, 12, 15, 29, 46–48, 51, 56–57, 127–28
    painful, 58
empathic listening, 124
empathy, xvi–xvii, 14–15, 117, 119, 121–24, 126–27, 129, 132, 135
employee assistance program (EAP), 33
employees
    high-caliber, 121
    high-potential, 120, 136
    remote, 53, 72–73
empowerment, 25, 73, 127
empower others, 17
energy, 10, 35–36, 53, 70, 75–76, 82
entanglements
    human, 107, 134
    knotted, 107
enthusiasm, 36, 74
environment
    hybrid, 13
    hybrid working, 14
    safe, 52, 126
    toxic, xx, 91
equality, xix, 88
equity, xxv, 86, 99–100
escalating conflict indicators, xv
ethnicities, 99, 109
exclusion, xv, 85–86
excuses, 28, 36

F

facial expressions, 51
fairness, xix, 88, 100, 134
faith, 36, 57, 59
fear, 30–31, 35, 37, 61, 76, 78, 103, 126–27
feedback, 29–31, 43–44, 49, 51–52, 73, 75–76, 78, 94–95

constructive, 51, 70, 78, 98
   regular, 73
feeling excluded, xxiii, 58, 86
fight-or-flight hormones, 28
First Nation community, 11
forgiveness, 7, 36, 72, 117
formal complaint, xi–xii, 18, 132
framework, ethical, 61, 79, 82
freedom, 30, 66, 89, 104, 111, 127
frustration, 31, 45, 86, 134
full power, 10, 12–13, 21

G
genders, 99
Goldgruber, Karin, 4
gossip, xix, 79, 90–91, 102–3
grace, 36, 121
great listeners, 45, 52
grief, 31, 126–27
groups, identity, 87
guilt, 31, 126

H
harassment, xii, 62
   personal, 62
   sexual, 62
hatred, 31
healing, 25, 31, 33, 87, 103
health crisis, xv
healthy teams, xvi–xvii, xxi, xxvi, 101, 134
high levels of innovation, xxv
HOLY SHIFT, xviii, 6–7, 37, 54, 57, 76, 91, 93
honesty, xiii, 34, 80, 94, 98, 123
hope, 30, 42, 44, 76, 96–97, 102, 106
HR managers, 13–14, 16, 35
human skills, 135
humbling blocks, 2, 34

humiliate, 62
humility, 34, 37, 77, 124

I
impartiality, 100
impatience, 31, 123
inclusion, xxv, 72, 86–87, 94–95, 99–100, 134
inclusive environment, 93
inner strength, developing, 32
inner work, 4, 7, 25, 104, 135
insecurities, xv, 3–4, 6, 31, 58, 65
integrity, 57, 59, 61, 65, 82, 88–89
intention
   good, 77, 82, 98, 108, 110, 114
   to respond, 39
   to understand, 39
interaction, emotional, 14
internal distractions, 43
interpersonal conflict, xxiii, 14, 93
interpersonal relationships, xv, 23, 78
interruptions, 43, 73
intimacy, 124
invalidating statements, 46
irritation, 31
isolation, xv, xxiii, 52

J
jealousy, xix, 31
job insecurity, xxv
journal, 8, 25, 31–32, 37, 106
journaling, 32, 136
joy, xx, 66–67, 97, 127
judgment, 39, 43–45, 48–51, 122, 128
justice, 100

K
keyboard warriors, xxv, 78, 132
kindness, 36
know thyself, 19

L

lack of
  communication, xxii–xxiii, 81, 88
  employee recognition, xxv
  integrity, 3
  productivity, xx
  resources, xix
  retention, xx
  team engagement, xx
  trust, xv, 52, 81, 89–90, 92
language, 60–61, 84, 99
leaders, good, 17, 120
leadership, 1, 52, 60, 75, 92, 120
  personal, 2, 136
  traits, 135
leadership development program,
  120
Leblanc, Lise, 102
lighten your load, xvi, 21–37, 132
limbic brain, 60–61
limiting beliefs, 3–4, 6–7, 9, 24,
  26–27, 37
listening, xii–xiii, 36, 39–45, 47,
  51–53, 71, 124
love, 34, 36, 41, 58, 60, 127, 129

M

managers, good, 17
manager tip, 67
McVanel, Sarah, 76
mediation, xiii, xx, xxvii, 7, 32-33,
  46–47, 87, 95, 97
  techniques, 90
mediator, 48, 51, 106
meeting rhythm, 53
meetings, closed-door, 92
memories, xix, 4–5, 22, 27
  earliest, 31
mental health, xxiv, 33, 136

Mental Health Commission of
  Canada, xxiv
mind wandering, 43
mirroring back, 44
misinterpretations, 34, 44, 132
mismanaged relationships, xx, xxiv
misunderstandings, 44, 125
model of communication, 42
momentum, 25, 36, 79
motivation, 61, 67, 75
motivational and leadership traits,
  135
multitasking, 39, 43

N

nationality, 99
need to FEEL understood, 41, 53,
  125
negativity, xix, xxii, 91, 102
negotiations, xviii, 44, 46–47, 64–65
  and conflict resolutions, 46
neurons, 22, 27, 29
neuroscientific theory, 22
next-highest thought, 127, 129, 135
nurture relationships, xvii, 69–84
nurturing, 69–71, 84, 101

O

offend, 62
organizational goals, 14
overwhelm, 31
overworked employees, xxv

P

pandemic, xv, xx, xxiv, xxvi, 92, 99,
  126. *See also* COVID-19
passion, 36, 55, 57, 59, 112
past psychological injury, 32
patient, 18, 79–80, 123, 132
patterning, old, 49

patterns, 22, 104
    old, 23, 33, 36
    of behavior, 31
people skills, 135
perception check, 82
perfect, xiv–xv, 15–16, 18, 123–24, 128–29, 136
perseverance, 13
personality
    differences, xxiii
    styles, 93, 109
    traits, 135
perspective, xii–xiii, 30, 35–36, 44, 47–50, 122, 124
    political, 99
    renewed, 36
pessimism, 31
Pew Research Center, 72
PLAY NICE, xvi, 96
poor management performance, xxv
Positive Pollys, 69, 78
potential, 13–14, 22, 24–26, 31–32, 36–37, 42–43, 49, 136
powerlessness, 31
Price, Ron, 97, 101
principles, xviii, 60, 84, 133
    of character, 34
pro-action, 12
problem solving, xviii, 17
process, consistent, 88
productive conversations, 46, 50
productive problem solvers, xvi, 131
productivity, xii, xx–xxi, 49, 52, 86, 93
professional development, 2
professional help, 33
profitable relationships, xviii, 25, 136
profits, xvii, xxvi, 81, 86, 126
promotions, xxiii, 14, 17, 19, 87–88, 136

psychological safety, 98, 126
psychotherapists, 33, 102

R
races, xvi, 99
rage, 31, 62, 103, 112
react, 10–11, 15
recognition, 35, 73–76, 78, 84, 133
    verbal, 70
recruitment process, 13
rejection, 12, 24
relationship challenges, 109, 111, 134
relationship potential, 105
relationships
    healthy, xvi, 46, 131
    nurturing, 69, 76, 78
relationship tools, xvi, 21, 132
religions, 99
remote work arrangements, xv
remote workers, 52, 72–73, 98
resilient, xxvi, 15, 58, 63, 120
resistance to change, xv, 56
resolution tools, xiv
resolving conflicts, xx, 59, 104
respect, 65, 67, 70–74, 77–78, 80, 84, 133
    mutual, 70, 80
responsibility
    employee's, 136
    employer's, 136
    taking, 2, 11, 16, 71, 103, 105–6
restating, 41, 47, 51
revenge, 31
roles
    employer's, xxi
    new, 14

S
Sandbox Strategies, xii–116, 120, 122, 124, 126, 128, 132, 134

Sandbox System, xii, 94
sandbox tool, 13
self-cultivation, 8, 19, 113
self-empathy, 123
self-reflection, 19, 34, 123
session
    brainstorming, 45
    leadership training, 59
setting healthy boundaries, 61, 65
Seven Grandfather Teachings, 34
sexual orientations, 99
sharing, xviii, 45, 72, 76, 83, 121–22
Sinek, Simon, 60
skills
    collaborative, xviii
    interdependence, 135
    interpersonal, 135
    social, xviii
social intelligence, 135
social stereotypes, 87
soft skills, 135
solid relationships, creating, 42
status, socioeconomic, 99
stories, old, 7–8, 21, 24–26, 28–30, 32, 35–37, 43
strategies
    inclusive, 86
    top-down, 86
stress, xix–xx, xxiii–xxiv, xxvi, 43–44, 73, 89, 91, 93
    high, xv
stress hormones, 28
stress leave, xix
stumbling blocks, 2, 34
subconscious programs, 33
substance use disorder (SUD), 116
success, xxvii, 1–19, 25, 71–73, 79, 129, 132

suitcase, 22–23, 25–27, 29–31, 36–37, 56, 58–59, 102–4. *See also* emotional baggage
sympathy, 121–22
synapse, 22, 27

T
take ownership, 12–13
take responsibility, xi, xvi, 18–19, 26, 50, 59
team
    conflict, 93, 112
    dysfunction, xx, 86
    engagement, xx, 77, 94
    meetings, 53, 89
    members, 14–15, 76, 88–90, 92, 112, 123
teamwork, 13–14, 17, 95, 121
therapy, 32, 104
the third story, 48–51
thought patterns, 4, 10, 22, 27–30
thoughts become things, 10, 19
three-bite rule, 107–8, 110, 117
time management, xxiii, 35-36
tolerance, 117, 123
tools, apology, 16, 129
toxic corporate culture, xxv
Tremblay Leadership Center, xv
trust, limited, xv
truth, 27, 34, 40, 123, 128, 135
twelve o'clock method of persistence, 11

U
unconscious emotions, identifying, 32
unconscious habits of thinking, 22
understand conflict, 46
understanding, 41–42, 45–48, 50, 54, 121–22, 124

unhealthy relationships, 110–11, 117, 134
unpack, 19, 21, 23, 29–33, 35, 75–76, 104, 132
unworthiness, 31

V
validate, 43, 45–46, 69, 73, 96, 110, 133
validation statements, 45
values, xv–xvi, 26, 71–72, 74, 81–84, 94, 115, 117
venting, 31, 90–91, 102
victim, 10, 62, 110
viewpoints, all-encompassing, 50
violence, lateral, 62
voice, assertive, xiv
vulnerability, xiii, 3, 7, 37, 122–24, 129

W
weaknesses, 3, 76, 125
WHY power, 55–56, 59, 61, 67–68, 71, 82

willpower, 56, 61, 133
wisdom, 34
workers, hybrid, 70
workload, xxiv
    fairness, xxii
    increased, xv
workplace
    bullying, 62
    conflict, xiv–xv, xx, xxii–xxiii, 91, 105
    culture, xii, 9, 50, 99, 102–3
    harassment, 62
    negative, xx
    relationships, 23, 54, 63
    sandbox, xviii, xx, 2, 11, 93, 99
    stress, xxiv–xxv
    success, 14
    toxic, xx, xxv
worksheet companion, 19, 54, 68, 84
    downloadable, 37
worry, 31, 44, 103, 128

Z
Zheng, Lily, 87

ACKNOWLEDGMENTS

I'M GRATEFUL FOR THE TEACHERS AND STUDENTS WHO GAVE INSIGHT and experiences to my career, which resound in stories and lessons that continue to play in my work. Navigating conflict on my own life path, I am so grateful for my family, good friends, and counselors.

Professor Samuel "Mooly" Dinnar from the Harvard Business School has been the type of professor who extends support and education long after you're in his class. I'm so grateful to have him affirm the value of this work by writing the foreword.

The list of those who contributed to this content is extensive, including Karin Goldgruber, Devin Metz, Tammy Dunnett, Monica Martin, Trent Theroux, Sarah McVanel, Mike Campigotto, Ron Price, Lise Leblanc, Sue LeBeau, Danielle Baker, and Mitch Paquette. The playful illustrations were created by my talented branding expert, Mandy Strang.

Asking for commitment letters and endorsements is easier when you have strong relationships, and I am blessed to have some longtime colleagues and new ones too who helped me review and endorse this work. Rosalind Lockyer, Corina Moore, Roy Slack, Greg Tumolo, Lise Leblanc, Trent Theroux, Barry Spilchuk, and Gary Furlong graciously gave the material a thumbs-up.

When COVID-19 canceled all speaking and training engagements, I used the unscheduled downtime to rewrite this manuscript to be relevant in a post-COVID world. Thank goodness my first call was to Dianna Booher, author and coach, to help me navigate the world of book proposals, agents, and publishers. Agent Dani Segelbaum of the Carol Mann Agency, editor Suzanne Staszak-Silva, indexer Nanette Norris, and all the hands that touched this work through the publisher Rowman & Littlefield are greatly appreciated.

ABOUT THE AUTHOR

PENNY TREMBLAY IS AN INTERNATIONAL SPEAKER, TRAINER, AND MEdiator. Founder of the Tremblay Leadership Center and the Sandbox System, Penny teaches people how to "play nice" in the sandbox at work, and when they don't, she helps them fix disconnected relationships.

Penny enjoys a spiritually connected life, great health, and strong relationships with her children and partner at her homes in North Bay, Ontario, and Riverside, Rhode Island. Her "Joy" is a yellow lab and the great outdoors, which balance the hours spent serving clients both in person and virtually across Canada and the United States.

Resources and Continuing Education

HOLY SHIFT Worksheet Companion: www.PennyTremblay.com /holyshift. Download to record action items while reading through all eight chapters.

SANDBOX STRATEGIES FOR THE NEW WORKPLACE

Find the following Keynotes and Sandbox Training programs at www.PennyTremblay.com:

PLAY NICE—Winning in the NEW Workplace Sandbox (for the entire team)

Relationships and Conflict Management—Managing in the NEW Workplace Sandbox (for managers and supervisors)

PLAY NICE—A Playful Approach to Resilience, Health, and Wellness (rooted in the Seven Grandfather Teachings)

CPSIA information can be obtained
at www.ICGtesting.com
Printed in the USA
BVHW041227150323
660151BV00001B/3